THE
RAILWAYS
OF GLASGOW

THE
RAILWAYS
OF GLASGOW

POST-BEECHING

GORDON D. WEBSTER

The
History
Press

Acknowledgements

In order to chronicle developments in Glasgow's railways within such a large timeframe (over fifty years) and with so many lines and stations to include, information had to be drawn from all nooks and crannies. I would like to thank the many people who went out of their way to help me with my research. Apologies in advance for anyone I may have accidentally left out: Craig Geddes from East Renfrewshire Council Archives; Angus MacDonald; Don Martin; Joseph McDermid, John Yellowlees and Martin Wyber from ScotRail; Donald Shankland; Milngavie Heritage Centre; the Mitchell Library, Glasgow; and the National Archives of Scotland.

I am especially grateful to those who contributed with photographs (and great railway knowledge too), from all different eras, which I would say all blend together perfectly: John Baker; Jules Hathaway; Tom Noble; Allan Trotter of Eastbank Model Railway Club; and of course my father, David Webster (whose photographs allowed me to come up with the idea of the Post-Beeching series in the first place). Lastly, thanks also to everyone at The History Press for the continued guidance.

Introduction

To most Glaswegians, the railway probably seems pretty insignificant, simply being a means of getting from A to B. Despite having resided in the city for a number of years, I myself admit to having taken it for granted at times. For a long time, I got used to the familiar routine of being able to turn up at Partick station whatever the time of day and be waiting no longer than a few minutes to catch a train into the city centre. Ten minutes later you would be in town and all without ever having to check a timetable. I also formerly stayed in Dunoon, which is much further away in deep Argyllshire and necessitates a boat journey too. But a seamless connection between the Caledonian MacBrayne ferry and

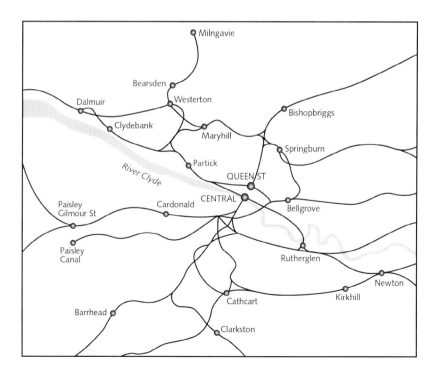

train at Gourock ensured you could travel up for a day in the city in an hour and ten minutes, which is very quick considering the change of transport. Going back was much the same, but for the wait in the bustling crowds at the Glasgow Central departure screen to discover which platform the train would depart from, typically 11,12 or 13.

But the facts about the railway speak for themselves. Glasgow has the most extensive suburban rail network in the UK outside London, serving a catchment area of more than 3 million people. It is a city steeped in railway history, most notably during the first half of the twentieth century, when it established itself as the locomotive building capital of the world. Steam engines were constructed by the North British Locomotive Company in Springburn and shipped from docks on the Clyde to destinations all over the continent.

The Garnkirk & Glasgow Railway became the city's first true railway when it started using steam locomotives in 1831, to transport coal into the city from the Monklands to the north. Standard-gauge line construction snowballed in the nineteenth century as more and more suburban passenger routes were added, as well as trunk routes which provided a vital link between the city and other towns or rural communities all over Scotland, not to mention Carlisle south of the border. Furthermore, Glasgow's physical and economic growth as a city was enhanced when the shipyards on the River Clyde got vital connecting rail links.

Class 303 EMU No. 303054 waits at Glasgow Central on 7 May 1986 with the 1305 Cathcart Inner Circle working. The unit carries Strathclyde PTE orange livery and has been refurbished, with headcode panels removed and hopper-type windows added. (Jules Hathaway)

As if this wasn't enough, the Glasgow Subway was constructed in 1896 and is now the third-oldest underground metro railway in the world. Much less well celebrated is the Glasgow Central low-level line, which has the distinction of being the most expensive sub-surface city line ever to be built. The navvies had to tunnel this route right underneath an already well-established city centre through the most solid rock, essentially fitting a railway around an existing community, unlike in some other areas where the railway got there first.

Glasgow's network of today is remarkably extensive, but different thanks to modernisation. This is partly due to Dr Richard Beeching's report *The Reshaping of British Railways*, published in 1963, which saw nearly a third of the UK's lines ruthlessly closed; undoubtedly an absolute watershed moment in railway history. The city's by then complex network would be significantly rationalised following the report, though, as we will see, there were to be some much more positive developments as well, sparked by revolutionary diesel and electric trains which replaced steam.

The Beeching Report targeted routes which were deemed to be unprofitable in the face of increased competition from road transport, leading to the abandonment of a number of branch lines which served communities in the suburbs of Glasgow. There were other more vital routes within the city itself which were seen as surplus to requirements, where there were already other neighbouring stations that served the same area on a different line, e.g. the closure of the Glasgow Central low-level line and Bridgeton Cross station, with Bridgeton Central still retained on a neighbouring route from Queen Street low-level. A more frequent and reliable bus service was also developing and this would spell the end for the Glasgow Corporation trams and trolleybuses too.

Rationalisation of Glasgow's railways was sparked not only by the Beeching Report but also British Railways' 1955 Modernisation Plan. Part of this was widespread electrification on main lines and suburban routes throughout the country, with Glasgow being one of the key areas that BR had pinpointed. The main benefits of electric trains would be improved acceleration and reliability; particularly ideal with the stop–start nature of inner-city services, which ran to very intensive timetables. Following this was a period of changing railway governance too, with a Passenger Transport Executive set up: first Greater Glasgow PTE, which later became Strathclyde PTE. ScotRail was also established as a brand for BR's Scottish Region, latterly becoming a train operating company in its own right following privatisation in 1994.

Taking into account all of the aforementioned history, it is surprising that so little has been written about Glasgow's railways, particularly chronicling the period since Beeching. I recently came to the conclusion that it merited some kind of up-to-date study, something which looks at all of the many developments that have happened since the 1960s. Everything that has happened in fifty years condensed into one book, so that those with a keen interest can easily find out about the railway without having to search lots of different sources, which was a problem that I had experienced myself.

Added to this, any existing media which has studied the city's railways has always looked at what most people regard as the golden age – the steam era. In the following pages, I have attempted to provide something of a bridge between this period and the present day that is reported in most magazines. Last but not least, the diesel and electric era seems to be of growing interest today. I believe that with the current generation, heritage diesel locomotives are fast becoming the new steam – you only need to look at the growth in the amount of diesels and BR 'corporate blue' livery across UK preserved lines.

As Glasgow is my home city, I felt blessed to have the opportunity to write this book and I especially enjoyed visiting all of the nooks and crannies of the city to capture the present-day photographs. The wet and murky weather seen on some of them will certainly be familiar to anyone who lives here! However, I don't really know why I decided to rely on twenty-year-old maps to get around the busy city roads, which proved to be something of a headache at times. Hindsight is a wonderful thing.

In the past few decades, the railway has faced stiff competition from a rapidly improved road network in Glasgow. On a foggy 10 January 2013, a ScotRail Class 320 EMU races alongside traffic on the Clydeside expressway near Finnieston. (Author's collection)

I wrote the first Post-Beeching title, about the West Highland lines, with a great emphasis on showcasing rural rail operations and beautiful scenery. Glasgow is, of course, very different, so I knew from the outset that this project would be a bit of fun. Here I set out with the aim of showing the exact opposite of what was in the previous release: trains in a busy city environment. I have tried throughout – and I do not mean this in a bad way – to show some of the urban grime and everyday city atmosphere that I feel makes Glasgow what it is, both in the text and the pictures.

It was interesting to note which particular stations in the region were recently suggested for possible closure by the Scottish Executive due to low passenger numbers, three of them being on the short Anniesland–Glasgow Queen Street line via Maryhill. Scaremongering media stories also implied that this route was being run down as there were no plans to electrify it. However, on the many times I have travelled on or visited the route in recent years, I never once saw a train arrive at a station where nobody boarded or alighted, even at quiet times such as weekday afternoons. At the end of the day, the Class 158 DMUs currently used are classified as 'Express' units, with a seating accommodation that is quite generous for a small branch line. I remember the days when long-distance Glasgow–Leeds and Inverness trains were two-car 158s!

The year 2014 is set to be a big one for Glasgow, with the Commonwealth Games being held in the city. It will also be a very important year for Scotland on the whole, as, together with the Games, there are the Homecoming events, the Ryder Cup golf tournament and – biggest of all – the independence referendum. As a result, all eyes will be on Glasgow and its transport system, and so within these pages I have tried to make reference to all of the specific improvement work that has gone into the railway in the run up.

With all of this in mind, make no mistake, 2014 is the year of Glasgow's railways. Additionally, last year marked the fiftieth anniversary of the Beeching Report so there is probably no better time to celebrate a Clydeside rail revival than now.

Gordon D. Webster
Glasgow, January 2014

Glossary

APT	Advanced Passenger Train
BR	British Rail
BRCW	Birmingham Railway Carriage & Wagon Company
BREL	British Rail Engineering Limited
BRML	British Rail Maintenance Limited
CR	Caledonian Railway
DBSO	driving brake second open
DEMU	diesel–electric multiple unit
DMU	diesel multiple unit
DRS	Direct Rail Services
DVT	driving van trailer
EMU	electric multiple unit
EWS	English Welsh & Scottish Railway
GBRf	GB Railfreight
GEKRDA	Glasgow–East Kilbride Railway Development Association
GGPTE	Greater Glasgow Passenger Transport Executive
GGTS	Greater Glasgow Transportation Survey
GSWR	Glasgow & South Western Railway
HST	High Speed Train
LMS	London, Midland & Scottish Railway
LNER	London & North Eastern Railway
NBL	North British Locomotive Company
NBR	North British Railway
PCI	Paisley Corridor Improvements
PTE	Passenger Transport Executive
RETB	Radio Electronic Token Block
SPT	Strathclyde Passenger Transport
SPTE	Strathclyde Passenger Transport Executive
SRPS	Scottish Railway Preservation Society
TMD	Traction Maintenance Depot
TOPS	Total Operations Processing System
TPO	travelling post office
WCML	West Coast Main Line

1

North Side

The south side of Glasgow has always had a vastly bigger network of lines than the north, with more of an emphasis on serving commuters. However, the north arguably has more of a distinctive railway history, as it was here that the two major railway companies in Scotland – the Caledonian Railway (CR) and North British Railway (NBR) – housed their overall construction works. The best known of these was the facility belonging to the North British Locomotive Company,

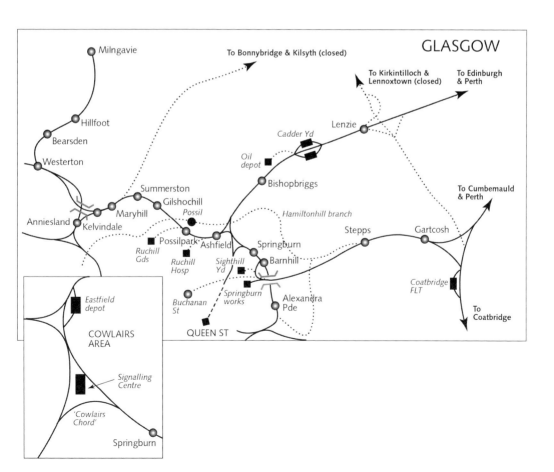

which became the largest of its kind in Europe, building locomotives for countries all across the world. Their main home was at Springburn, near to the CR and NBR's sizeable plants at St Rollox and Cowlairs.

Glasgow Buchanan Street and Glasgow Queen Street were the original two main termini serving trains to the north, operated by the Caledonian Railway and North British Railway respectively. These two companies dominated the lines at this side of the city until 1923, when they became the London, Midland & Scottish Railway (LMS) and the London & North Eastern Railway (LNER). The principal routes were the LNER's Glasgow–Edinburgh main line and the LMS' line north to Stirling via Cumbernauld. The LNER gained control of most of the north side suburban network from the North British, which included the Cowlairs–Westerton section used by West Highland Line trains to and from Glasgow Queen Street.

The Glasgow rail network of today reveals that many routes eventually terminate at some point, being essentially branch lines. However, the north side is still mostly made up of through-routes like it used to be, joined together at each end by various connecting junctions. The North British branch from Westerton to Milngavie was the only major route which came to a buffer stop. It was at Milngavie, in June 1930, that the George Bennie Railplane invention was brought to life. A small demonstration track was erected to showcase this curious monorail-like form of transport for a short period, though it failed to develop any further and was abandoned after the war.

The BR 1955 Modernisation Plan saw diesel traction fast becoming established all over the country, though in Glasgow it was electric multiple units that would sound the death knell for a lot of the steam-hauled suburban trains. Overhead catenary was erected along the length of the North Clyde line, from Balloch Pier and Helensburgh Central to Milngavie, Springburn, Airdrie and Bridgeton Central in the north and east.

In November 1960, Class 303 EMUs took over from steam, but only lasted for a few weeks before the entire fleet had to be withdrawn en masse due to transformer faults. Amazingly the steam-hauled trains returned, running 'under the wires' for nearly a full year on the North Clyde route before the problems with the 303s were ironed out and they re-entered traffic, this time for good.

The Class 303s proved very popular with passengers and soon earned the nickname 'The Blue Trains' as a result of their unique Caledonian Railway-style blue colour scheme. Electrification itself was seen as the way forward for Glasgow's suburban network, allowing faster, more efficient operations without the maintenance issues associated with steam locomotives. Eliminating steam from the underground section of the North Clyde route through Glasgow Queen Street low-level and Charing Cross certainly went some way towards making it a brighter and cleaner environment, and therefore improving the city's image.

The secondary routes and branches in the north of the city were inevitably going to be under close scrutiny with the publishing of the Beeching Report in 1963. There had already been major cutbacks in recent years to some of the rural sections of line that stretched into the Trossachs and Campsie hills to the north, including part of the route from Lenzie Junction to Aberfoyle. By the late 1950s, the line had closed to both passenger and freight west of Kirkintilloch; the line south of there was still served by passenger traffic from Glasgow Queen Street and freight.

The remaining 1½-mile section from Lenzie Junction to Kirkintilloch became an early casualty of Beeching, which closed after its last passenger train in September 1964. Within the city itself, a major cutback shortly after was the closure of all of the ex-CR low-level lines which stretched from Dalmuir Riverside in the west to Coatbridge Central in the east. This included the line from Partick West to Maryhill Central and Possil, which saw its last passenger trains in October 1964. Maryhill's other station – Maryhill Park – had closed in October 1961, though the line through here between Cowlairs and Westerton remained open for West Highland Line workings. In addition, the branch lines to Ruchill Goods and Ruchill Hospital closed in July 1963.

April 1966 saw the closure of what remained of the former Kelvin Valley Railway from Maryhill to Bonnybridge and Kilsyth, by that time only served by occasional freight. The north Glasgow rail network was therefore already looking quite skeletal by the time BR announced the closure of Buchanan Street station – the most significant yet. This sizeable terminus shut on 7 November 1966, with its remaining main line services transferring to Queen Street.

Generally regarded as the least aesthetically pleasing of the four main termini in the city, Buchanan Street had been the terminus for services to Inverness, Dundee, Aberdeen and Oban via Callander. It is probably best known for its final few years of existence, when it was served by the three-hour Glasgow–Aberdeen expresses hauled by Sir Nigel Gresley's famous A4 Pacifics in their swansong years. Additionally, there was a large neighbouring goods depot on the same site until 1962.

As at Queen Street, the line out of Buchanan Street had to burrow underground on a significant gradient to reach the northern suburbs of the city. Following closure and the clearing of the station site here, the land was soon redeveloped, with Buchanan bus station and Glasgow Caledonian University eventually occupying the area, along with ScotRail's offices on Port Dundas Road (ScotRail House). The only real traces of the station remaining today are the tunnel mouth and retaining walls from the approach lines, which are visible behind a block of student flats adjacent to the M8 motorway.

Significant track rationalisation took place around the Springburn and St Rollox district following not only the Beeching closures, but the demise of

A surviving tunnel portal seen today near the site of Glasgow Buchanan Street station, closed in 1966. (Author's collection)

the locomotive works in the area. The North British Locomotive Company (NBL) had latterly suffered from major financial problems, following the lack of success of some of its diesel and electric locomotives built for BR, such as the Scottish-allocated Class 29s. These would be one of the last types of locomotive that that the company would ever produce. If anything, the NBL's plight at this time typified the current trend of Glasgow and the west of Scotland losing its grip as one of the engineering strongholds of the world.

The NBL was dissolved in 1962, followed in 1968 by the closure of the neighbouring ex-NBR Cowlairs works. All future major repairs were concentrated on the ex-CR plant at St Rollox, which was by now BR's primary locomotive and rolling stock works facility in Scotland, named British Rail Engineering Ltd (BREL) Springburn. BREL's presence here, together with that of the massive Eastfield Motive Power Depot and marshalling yards at Cadder and Sighthill, ensured that railway traditions stayed strong in this side of the city, though there was further industrial decline to the north, where the remaining coal mines were closed, such as the Twechar and Gartshore pits near the Forth & Clyde Canal.

Other changes saw the freight line from Townhead and St Rollox removed in 1968, resulting in a much simplified route between Cowlairs and Gartcosh Junction, near Coatbridge. The only passenger trains still in use over this section became Springburn–Cumbernauld DMU shuttles. Cumbernauld was one of Scotland's 'new towns', built in the 1950s to combat poor housing and over-population in the city following the Second World War. Cumbernauld station had been there since 1848, though the railway did not play as pivotal a role in the town's development as it could have. The station ended up being located slightly too far away from the town centre and has generally struggled to compete with the town's growing road network ever since.

Following the 1960s, Glasgow on the whole benefited from significant investment in roads, while the railway took something of a back seat, with no further electrification or rolling stock improvements except that of the West Coast Main Line to the south. The 1945 Bruce Report had sparked major transport regeneration projects, mainly large-scale road building, though most of these were long term, only truly beginning to take hold after the 1960s. The Glasgow–Edinburgh M8 and Glasgow–Stirling M80 motorways were the most notable, though the work took decades to complete after beginning in the 1960s.

A six-car formation of Class 126 DMUs passes Woodilee, near Lenzie, with an Edinburgh Waverley–Glasgow Queen Street express in December 1968. The fifth coach is still in BR green livery. (Allan Trotter, Eastbank Model Railway Club)

In terms of public transport, the report would later result in the building of two major bus stations in Glasgow: Anderston and Buchanan Street, opening in 1972 and 1977 respectively. The report's suggested rail improvements, made long before Beeching, included closing all four main termini (Buchanan Street, Queen Street, St Enoch and Central) to be replaced by two – 'Glasgow North' and 'Glasgow South'. Beeching's own plans had at least saved two of them.

The building of the M8 motorway between Glasgow and Edinburgh put extra pressure on the railways to compete with the roads. Swindon Cross-Country Class 126 DMUs had taken over from steam locomotives on the Glasgow–Edinburgh line in the late 1950s, but by the late 1960s many people had reservations about their suitability for the route. To allow for a faster and more reliable service, a return to locomotive haulage was made.

BRCW Class 27s would take over the services in May 1971, with one locomotive at each end of the train working in push–pull formation, hauling rakes of six Mark 2 coaches. The 27s had been in regular use on the West Highland routes out of Queen Street since 1962, where they had very much endeared themselves to the crews. The transfer of further locomotives to Eastfield

On the eastern approach to Cadder Yard on the Edinburgh–Glasgow route, Class 29 No. D6137 has just propelled a mixed goods working out on to the main line and now leaves on its journey west. Taken in August 1971, this is possibly one of the last views of a NBL Type 2 in service and D6137 was one of only a handful to carry BR blue livery. (Allan Trotter, Eastbank Model Railway Club)

depot allowed them to begin work on the Glasgow–Edinburgh shuttles, where an intensive 90mph service was introduced. The higher speeds shortened journey times from fifty-five minutes to as little as forty-three.

The Greater Glasgow Transportation Survey (GGTS) published the first of a series of reports in 1968, led by a steering committee that included members of Glasgow Corporation Transport and British Rail. As well as road transport, rail development in the city was a key part of the agenda, and this was set out further in four more reports published between 1968 and 1974. These put forward a series of recommendations for line and rolling stock improvements, which were to be completed by 1985. When putting the proposals together, the steering committee took into account factors such as anticipated car use, population and employment figures by 1990.

Unfortunately some of the GGTS' forecasted figures eventually turned out to be wide of the mark, especially with population steadily declining after the 1960s. Nevertheless, those transport proposals which did get carried out would eventually prove to be a success, though one which never got off the ground involved a curious reversal of the Beeching axe to reopen the branch line to Kirkintilloch for passengers. It was suggested that this could be electrified, with the wires now extending all the way from Springburn through Lenzie. Less than a decade after the branch had been shut, the folly of some of Beeching's closures was already being realised.

There were plans to electrify both the Motherwell–Cumbernauld line via Coatbridge and the extension to Springburn via Stepps, with a 'Garngad chord' that would provide an east-facing link between the latter line and the North Clyde route to Airdrie. Furthermore, the Hyndland–Maryhill Central–Possil route was to reopen as well as the long-closed Hamiltonhill branch through Springburn, including new stations at Kelvindale, Milton, Stobhill and Red Road. These too were to be electrified. All of the recommended route and station reopenings were to be carried out between 1978 and 1985.

The Greater Glasgow Passenger Transport Executive (GGPTE) was created in 1973 and became responsible for co-ordinating all public transport throughout the city, the train services being operated by BR on the PTE's behalf. An immediate priority was to relay the old 'Caley' Glasgow Central low-level route between Stobcross and Rutherglen, as the new 'Argyle line', which finally opened in November 1979. However, plans to restore the original extension to Maryhill and Possil did not come to fruition.

Most of the other projects set out in the GGTS reports for line reinstatements would also gradually fall by the wayside, for now anyway. Strathclyde PTE took over transport operations in 1980 from Greater Glasgow and gradually applied its distinctive orange and black livery not only to trains (including on the Glasgow Subway), but also to buses. As such, Glasgow soon had its own distinctive brand

May 1971 saw Class 126 DMUs replaced on the Glasgow–Edinburgh circuit by Class 27 diesels working in push–pull mode. No. 27112 is pictured leading the 1330 Edinburgh–Glasgow down the Cowlairs Incline on 22 August 1977. (Tom Noble)

that separated it from anywhere else in the UK, helped by bright marketing campaigns to boot.

Various classes of DMU and EMU were repainted with the SPTE livery, with the legend 'Strathclyde Transport' printed on the bodysides. Previous blue and grey examples had carried the words 'GG Trans-Clyde' (GG for Greater Glasgow). In September 1983, Strathclyde Transport essentially became the Glasgow operating wing of ScotRail. ScotRail was the new brand name given to BR's Scottish Region and this too was adopted on the sides of trains; namely the blue-and-grey-liveried DMUs and Mark 1, 2 and 3 carriages.

ScotRail also developed a vast array of marketing schemes which would breathe new life into railways north of the border. This included a new version of the InterCity livery (with a light blue stripe) for use on the Glasgow–Edinburgh expresses, which added further variation following a long period of monotony with BR's 'corporate blue' colour scheme. The Glasgow–Edinburgh circuit had begun using air-conditioned Mark 2 and 3 coaches in 1979, when the life-expired Class 27s started to be replaced with Class 47s. Twelve 47s were specially converted into the sub-class 47/7 to run in push–pull mode, with a locomotive at one end and a DBSO (driving brake second open) vehicle at the other.

The same trains also commenced operation on the Glasgow–Aberdeen route in 1985, when another four 47/7s were added to the fleet.

December 1983 saw a proposal to have the whole Bellgrove–Springburn–Cumbernauld section closed to passenger traffic, with Cumbernauld only served via the Coatbridge line. This plan was aborted later in the decade after concern grew over the large scale of unemployment and deprivation in the north-east corner of the city, with the city council concluding that removing rail links would make this even worse.

Another pleasing development was the reinstatement of services between Glasgow city centre and Cumbernauld, when the half-hourly Springburn–Cumbernauld shuttle was extended to work from Glasgow Queen Street high-level on 15 May 1989. New stations were opened along the route at Greenfaulds (near Cumbernauld) and Stepps. Trains were required to reverse at Cowlairs, as the Cowlairs–Springburn spur still joined the main line into Queen Street at a north-facing junction.

All over the BR network, the late 1980s into the early 1990s saw the widespread introduction of 'second-generation' DMUs – in this case the Class 156 Sprinter and Class 158 Express Sprinter types. Loco-hauled trains were the first to go, and by late 1990 Queen Street station had become virtually a locomotive-free zone. 'First-generation' DMUs, chiefly classes 101 and 107, would also hand the last of their local duties from Dunblane and Falkirk Grahamston over to 156s and 158s the following year.

Today, the Milngavie branch is unusually busy for a route that is partly single track. On 19 March 2009, SPT carmine and cream-liveried 320311 *Royal College of Physicians and Surgeons of Glasgow* awaits departure from Milngavie. Note the beautifully preserved station building and canopy. (Author's collection)

Single track to Milngavie

In 1989, BR proposed altering the double track Westerton–Milngavie branch to single line for most of its length. The move sparked a furious reaction from locals, who argued that it would jeopardise safety at Westerton Junction (formerly named Milngavie Junction), where the branch diverged away from the Queen Street–Helensburgh main line. The 1989 Bellgrove accident (see page 42) had demonstrated the risk of collisions at single-lead junctions in the event of a signal being passed at danger. BR had implemented this sort of simplified layout at various locations in a bid to cut costs. The safety risk it posed was highlighted by the Single Track Action Group, which was formed to stop the Milngavie project going ahead.

A petition supported by local MPs and community councils, with 5,200 signatures, was submitted to BR to persuade them to cancel the plans. This was unsuccessful, and late in 1990 the track singling project eventually went ahead. The railway became single line the whole way from Westerton Junction to Milngavie, apart from a short section between Bearsden and just north of Hillfoot where double track was retained, while resignalling also took place.

A higher service frequency along the branch would follow in later years. While this benefited passengers, the lack of flexibility offered by single line working was soon very clear to see.

The end of loco-haulage and decline of local freight would subsequently result in the closure of Eastfield locomotive depot in November 1992. Many locomotives were transferred to Motherwell depot, near to the large marshalling yard at Mossend, which had taken over from the now closed yards at Cadder and Sighthill. A new incarnation of Eastfield depot would subsequently appear in 2004 for servicing DMUs.

Meanwhile, 23 September 1993 saw the opening of the 'Cowlairs chord' – a new spur to allow through-running between Glasgow Queen Street and Cumbernauld without trains having to reverse (consequently cutting the thirty-three-minute journey time by eight minutes). It connected with the existing Cowlairs–Springburn spur to form a second triangular junction at Cowlairs.

Residents in the north of the city received a further boost on 2 December that year, when passenger services returned to Maryhill. A new Maryhill station was opened on the site of the old one at Maryhill Park, with a DMU shuttle service running between there and Queen Street high-level. New intermediate stations were also constructed at Ashfield, Possilpark and Parkhouse, Lambhill (renamed

On Sunday 22 July 1990, Class 150 Sprinter No. 150284 leads a Class 156 on the 1122 Glasgow–Aberdeen service near Provanmill, diverted via Cumbernauld due to engineering work on the Edinburgh and Glasgow main line. In the background is a new bridge recently built across the Stepps bypass road. Its construction had seen the trackbed moved over slightly; the old formation can be seen to the right. (Tom Noble)

Gilshochill in 1998) and Summerston. The new services shared this section of line with West Highland trains (none of which called at the new stations), which remained double track throughout.

Under the new franchise following privatisation, ScotRail paid particular attention to improving commuter travel, including the installation of more park-and-ride facilities around the city's suburbs. In 2011, a 700-space park-and-ride was opened at Croy station; an addition to its existing 215-space car park. This made it the largest of its kind anywhere on the ScotRail network.

The introduction of Class 170 Turbostar DMUs on the Glasgow–Edinburgh circuit was another step in the same direction, with trains running – for the very first time – to an intensive fifteen-minute frequency. A massive growth in passenger numbers along this route meant that overcrowding became a problem during peak hours, though this was partly alleviated with more Turbostars doubling up into six-car formations. The Edinburgh and Glasgow line soon became widely recognised as ScotRail's flagship route, such were the levels of investment being put into it, and it has not stopped there; the Edinburgh to Glasgow Improvement Programme is currently underway to provide a further improved service by 2016. The work will result in the electrification of the route, which is expected to offer increased journey times and, eventually, eight-coach trains.

Happily, the post-millennium era saw further Beeching reversals in the north, with Strathclyde Passenger Transport (SPT) and ScotRail working together to build a seamless transport network that would get people off the busy city roads and on to public transport. Gartcosh station – closed back in November 1962 – was reopened on 9 May 2005, on the Springburn–Cumbernauld route. The new station was funded by SPT, the Scottish Executive and North Lanarkshire Council and served by a half-hourly Glasgow–Cumbernauld service mostly using SPT's small fleet of Class 170s. The station lay next to an industrial park, built on the site of the former British Steel works. A few years later plans also re-emerged for the nearby 'Garngad chord' link proposed back in the 1970s, only for it to die on the vine once again.

Later that year, on 28 September, Queen Street–Maryhill diesel services were extended to run into Anniesland, where a new bay platform was built at the current station on the electrified North Clyde line. This saw the rebuilding of a

Kelvindale was an all new station opened in 2005 and has a true branch line atmosphere despite being in an urban location. On 16 December 2013, 158717 calls with the 1051 Anniesland–Glasgow Queen Street. (Author's collection)

mile-long section of track between Maryhill Park Junction and Anniesland, with a new intermediate station opened at Kelvindale. There had been no passenger service along there since before the First World War, but a reinstatement had been planned for a long time. Strathclyde PTE had hoped to reach Anniesland back in 1993 but ended up only going as far as Maryhill. Kelvindale station itself was initially going to be named Dawsholm.

Before this new half-hourly service was brought in, Queen Street–Maryhill trains had to run to Westerton to cross lines and reverse. Running into Anniesland would provide a valuable interchange with the electric services, but no junction was laid there to connect the two lines. This was a very strange move, especially as a connection would have allowed for future north–south Crossrail links.

Incredibly, Kelvindale was actually suggested for closure a few years later in January 2012, along with another eight railway stations in Glasgow which were said to suffer from low passenger usage. This included others in the northern half of the city at Ashfield, Barnhill, Gilshochill and Maryhill, which were pinpointed because there were neighbouring stations within a one-mile radius providing the same service. A Transport Scotland consultation explored the option of closing them, stating this would save £208,000 per annum. Mercifully, this was ruled out a couple of months later, when Transport Minister Keith Brown revealed they would not be shut following a successful 'Save Our Stations' campaign by the *Evening Times* newspaper, backed by local politicians.

2

South Side

Lines south of the Clyde were originally the territory of the Caledonian Railway and Glasgow & South Western Railway (GSWR). The 'Caley's' Glasgow Central–Carlisle section of the West Coast Main Line was the principal express route, with the GSWR working their own competing main line, the Nith Valley route via Dumfries. While the CR operated out of Central station, the GSWR had their own large terminus a stone's throw away along the Broomielaw at Glasgow St Enoch. As at Central, the approach lines here crossed a bridge over the Clyde, south of which a network of lines connected the two. In 1923 both companies joined the London, Midland & Scottish Railway (LMS), which thereafter controlled all lines in the south-west.

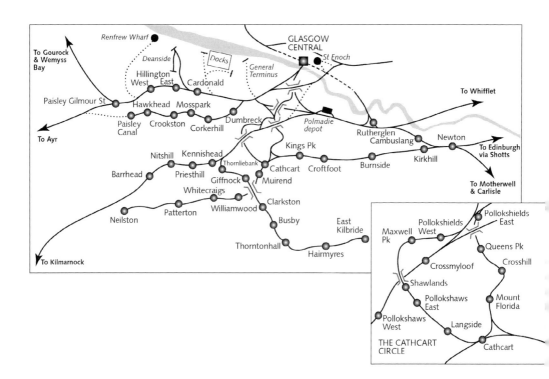

The LMS' sphere of operations in the south side was very large and most routes continue in passenger use today. The dormitory towns of Neilston and East Kilbride were both served via branch lines, while trains to Newton, Motherwell, Lanark and Edinburgh (on the line via Shotts) shared use of the West Coast Main Line with the crack Glasgow–London Euston expresses to the outskirts of the city. The most prestigious trains were the Coronation Scot, Royal Scot and Caledonian services to London, using, for many years, Sir William Stanier's powerful 'Duchess' Pacifics. The Royal Scot title lasted long into the electric era; the southbound working always departing Central at around 10 a.m. each day at the same time as its corresponding service from Euston.

The double track Cathcart Circle line was used by frequent commuter services to the leafy tenement-lined suburbs in the south, with no less than ten stations along its 5½-mile length. It became famous for handling large numbers of football specials to Mount Florida, for Hampden Park. To the west lay the GSWR main line to Kilmarnock and Carlisle via Barrhead, as well as two routes towards Paisley and the Clyde coast (one via Paisley Canal and the other over the CR–GSWR Joint line via Paisley Gilmour Street) which converged at Elderslie.

Nationalisation and the 1955 Modernisation Plan brought about inevitable changes in rolling stock, firstly with various types of first-generation DMUs being introduced on local services. The Glasgow south side electrification scheme followed after the north side in May 1962, when the Cathcart Circle and its connecting routes to Neilston and Motherwell (via Kirkhill and Newton) were the first to be converted. In public timetables, BR gave special mention to which routes were included in the 'Blue Train Service' network, while other services into Lanarkshire serving the Hamilton Circle line and Lanark itself were 'Green Train' services, as they used DMUs.

The proposal to build a 'Glasgow South' station to replace both Central and St Enoch (outlined in the 1945 Bruce Report) was not a feasible rationalisation option, but BR felt they could no longer justify having two large south-facing termini in such close proximity. Beeching's axe would ultimately fall on St Enoch, which closed to passenger traffic on 27 June 1966, with all its services being transferred to Central. The fact that it was still served by 250 trains to destinations all over the west coast and south of the border and was used by 23,000 passengers per weekday, was not enough to save it, with the counter-argument being that its destinations could be just as easily served from Central.

St Enoch would still be served by parcels trains until complete closure on 5 June 1967, though the main structure would survive intact, used as a car park, for a number of years before being demolished completely a decade later following the closure of the adjoining St Enoch hotel. The St Enoch Centre shopping complex now occupies the site, though a number of the station's approach embankments are still in situ. The 1899-built City Union bridge still survives

Glasgow St Enoch terminus is seen during its last month of operation in June 1966, with Corkerhill-based Standard Class 5 No. 73100 awaiting departure on a southbound excursion, complete with non-corridor suburban carriages. Today, barely a trace of the station remains. (Allan Trotter, Eastbank Model Railway Club)

to carry the north–south connecting line through the Gorbals (the City Union line), which continued in use for freight and empty coaching stock workings after St Enoch's closure.

Glasgow Central low-level station shut on 5 October 1964 along with the rest of the stations on the old CR line from Dalmuir Riverside. This included the Bridgeton–Rutherglen and Bridgeton–Carmyle sections of line. Although other south side suburban routes survived the Beeching axe, a few were initially proposed for closure but were retained as common sense prevailed. The ex-CR route to Edinburgh via Shotts and the GSWR main line to Kilmarnock were both reprieved as such. Meanwhile, the East Kilbride branch was also threatened despite its link to one of Scotland's ever-growing 'new towns'. This resulted in the formation of the Glasgow–East Kilbride Railway Development Association (GEKRDA) in November 1963, whose hard work eventually paid off when this line was also saved.

The decline of shipbuilding along the Clyde resulted in the closure of the Ibrox Junction–Govan branch in June 1966, which ran on to the nearby docks and was served by regular freight traffic. Ibrox station, on the main line from Glasgow

Central to Paisley Gilmour Street, was closed eight months later, despite still being well-used by numerous football specials running to Rangers FC's nearby stadium. Furthermore, the four-track main line through there, extending from Shields Junction to Paisley Gilmour Street, was cut down to two tracks in 1966. The two middle 'fast' lines were removed to accommodate the overhead catenary being installed on the route as far as Gourock and Wemyss Bay.

Further west along the river, passenger services ceased on the line from Arkleston Junction, Paisley, to Renfrew Wharf on 5 June 1967, the same day that electric services were inaugurated between Glasgow Central–Gourock/Wemyss Bay. Friday 28 April had seen the very last steam-hauled passenger train operate on BR's Scottish Region, when LMS Fairburn 2-6-4 tank No. 42274 hauled the 1703 Gourock–Glasgow. English-based locomotives still visited Scotland occasionally until the year was out, but other than that, steam was gone.

Local transport authorities took a very different attitude towards the railway than BR under Dr Beeching. Just as the dust was settling following the Beeching cuts, the first Greater Glasgow Transportation Survey in 1968 planned reinstatements of some of the very lines which had closed. The biggest priority was to reinstate the Glasgow Central low-level route, closed only four years earlier! Furthermore, the Steering Committee wanted the electrification of near enough every passenger route to south of the Clyde, with new stations to boot.

New stations proposed included Gallowhill (between Hillington and Paisley), Hawkhead and Bellahouston (both on the line via Paisley Canal). It was also suggested that East Kilbride could have its station moved closer to the town centre, with the line being electrified along with Glasgow–Barrhead. The Barrhead–Kilmarnock section was outlined for closure. One major step forward would involve the reopening of the City Union line through the Gorbals to passenger services, to allow a north–south connection across the Clyde. Both west- and east-facing junctions would now join this to the North Clyde line near Bellgrove, with another new junction laid to join the North Clyde to the Central low-level route.

By the dawn of the 1970s, electrification of the West Coast Main Line (WCML) was gathering pace, gradually extending northwards after London–Crewe went 'under the wires' first during the 1960s. The introduction of new English Electric Class 50 diesels to passenger services in 1967 would just be a stop-gap measure until the Scottish section was electrified. During this period, Anglo-Scottish expresses were regularly diverted over the GSWR main line via Dumfries when the WCML north of Carlisle was closed, while part-closures around Glasgow also saw them routed via the Cathcart Circle. A figure in the region of £38 million was spent on route enhancements north of Crewe, which included complete resignalling, whilst another £36 million was spent just on the electrification itself.

BR blue-and-grey-liveried Class 311 unit No. 311108 arrives at Cathcart with a Glasgow Central–Neilston working, on 14 November 1983. The western connecting line from Kirkhill, seen on the extreme right, bypasses the station and joins the Cathcart Circle behind the camera at Cathcart West Junction, where the branch to Neilston also diverges. (Tom Noble)

Electric services started over the full WCML from Glasgow on 6 May 1974, with new Class 87 locomotives, nicknamed the 'Electric Scots', taking over services. It would see London–Glasgow journey times reduced to as little as five hours compared to the Class 50s' six hours (itself a new record back in 1970). A special ceremony at Glasgow Central the following day saw Her Majesty the Queen, accompanied by HRH The Duke of Edinburgh, make a special visit to inaugurate the new trains. The Royal Train had transported them north from Preston that day, making various stops for special presentations along the way, including at Oxenholme and Carstairs, where the Duke of Edinburgh climbed onboard the Class 87 for a cab ride to Motherwell. At Shields Road depot, the royal party were given a tour of the facilities, where some of the WCML electrics would be maintained.

Meanwhile, on the city's suburban network, the only one of the aforementioned elaborate reopening proposals made by the GGTS that did get taken forward within the expected timescale, apart from the Central low-level route, was the electrification of the Hamilton Circle. It was electrified at the same time as the WCML and the branch line to Lanark, and from November 1979 was served by trains on the reinstated Central low-level 'Argyle line'.

Previously earmarked for electrification at an estimated cost of £1.9 million, the Glasgow Central–Kilmacolm via Paisley Canal route was becoming a major loss-maker for BR. The first major Glasgow line closure since Beeching, the line lost its passenger service on 10 January 1983 and track was lifted a few years later along the short branch from Elderslie to Bridge of Weir and Kilmacolm. This resulted in the loop line through Paisley Canal being cut back from its westernmost junction at Elderslie to become little more than a branch line serving Hawkhead oil terminal and Corkerhill depot. Previously it had been a diversionary route from the main line through Paisley Gilmour Street, even on its very last day before closure, when engineering work saw Glasgow–Ayr/Stranraer trains rerouted along there for the very last time.

Fast forward to 1987, and lo and behold plans were afoot to reopen the line for passengers as far as Paisley Canal! City of Glasgow District Council were worried about further potential closures on suburban lines and the drastic effect this would have on the surrounding communities. They touched on many of the same plans put forward by the GGTS two decades previously, such as electrification and station reinstatements.

Fast and frequent electric services started along Glasgow–Ayr on 29 September 1986, when the route south of Paisley Gilmour Street was electrified, with DMUs being replaced by Class 318 EMUs. Another relatively new type seen in Glasgow alongside them were the Class 314s, having been brought into service on the new Argyle line in 1979. Strathclyde PTE then invested further in new trains when Class 156 Sprinters and Class 320s were introduced in 1988 and 1990 respectively. The latter class would work the North Clyde route, further strengthening the EMU fleet and meaning there didn't have to be the same level of reliance on the ageing Class 303 'Blue Trains'.

On 26 November 1987, three-car Class 101 DMU No. 101329 arrives at Hairmyres, with the 1320 East Kilbride–Glasgow Central. (David Webster)

East Kilbride: The branch that refused to die

Much has been published about successful local campaigns that saved some of Britain's scenic rural lines when they were threatened with closure; the Settle and Carlisle route being a prime example. Much less well known is the fight that took place to save the Glasgow–East Kilbride route, successfully led by the Glasgow–East Kilbride Railway Development Association (GEKRDA). The line was seriously threatened with the chop not just under Beeching, but later at the start of the 1980s as well. The leaders of the association, the late Jack and Helen Broadbent, essentially had a fight on their hands for over two decades and ultimately helped to secure a faster and much more frequent service in 1989, using Sprinters.

The route itself managed to remain relatively unchanged through the years despite two major rationalisation plans. The first, proposed by BR and Strathclyde Regional Council in 1983, was to close the line west of Clarkston and build a new junction from Muirend on the Glasgow–Neilston branch, thereby closing Thornliebank and Giffnock stations. The Neilston branch was also to close to the south. But pressure from GEKRDA saw the whole plan eventually scrapped. Furthermore, a new East Kilbride terminus closer to the town centre was expected to be built later in the 1980s to replace the present station to the north. This too was cancelled, after opposition from local residents who feared their homes would be demolished to make way for the new half-mile line extension.

The 7½-mile East Kilbride branch originally ran as far as Busby only; hence Busby Junction is the name given to the point where it diverges from the Glasgow and South Western main line. Following Beeching, the line has remained double track as far as Busby station, with a single track section to the east, though the expanded timetable of 1989 saw a passing loop installed between Hairmyres and East Kilbride to boost capacity.

1990 saw an all new station opened in the south of the city at Priesthill and Darnley on the Glasgow–Barrhead route, on 23 April. Better still, passenger services were then reinstated between Glasgow Central and Paisley Canal on 27 July, using Sprinters. Paisley Canal received a brand-new station of its own, only yards away from the previous one, which had been bulldozed into a car park with its former building now used as a pub. Along the 6-mile line from Shields Junction, a new station was added at Dumbreck, to join those reopened at Corkerhill, Mosspark and Crookston. Passenger services officially began on 30 July 1990, though the previous two days had seen a special reduced-fare service operated for local residents. A new Hawkhead station was later opened on 12 April 1991 to serve a residential area on the outskirts of Paisley.

1991 is often sadly remembered for the accident at Newton, when a head-on collision between two electric trains resulted in four fatalities on the evening of 21 July. The 2155 Newton–Glasgow service had just left Newton station when it was believed to have passed the platform starting signal at danger, subsequently running straight into the path of the 2055 Balloch–Motherwell service at the single-lead junction towards Kirkhill. As well as the death of both trains' drivers, two passengers lost their lives while another twenty-two were injured. An inquiry concluded that the accident could have been avoided had the junction at Newton not been of a single-lead arrangement. A new double-lead junction was hastily installed in its place in the immediate aftermath.

A previous accident back in 1979 at Paisley Gilmour Street – similar in that its primary cause was a signal passed at danger – had seen two trains collide head-on at the eastern approaches to the station, claiming the lives of seven people (both drivers and five passengers) and injuring sixty-seven. On the evening of 16 April, the 1858 Ayr–Glasgow special service, made up of two Class 126 DMUs, passed a red signal upon departure from platform 2 and hit the 1940 Glasgow–Wemyss Bay (2 X Class 303) at the crossover where the Ayr and Inverclyde lines converge. New safety measures have since been installed on the railways as a direct result of accidents such as those at Paisley and Newton (and Bellgrove in 1989, examined on page 42). The Train Protection and Warning System(TPWS), implemented all across the country just after the new millennium, now ensures that brakes are automatically activated on a train that is overspeeding or has passed a red signal, significantly reducing the chances of a collision or derailment.

Station and line reopenings were still high on the agenda for Strathclyde PTE through the 1990s, and early in the decade consideration was already being given to electrifying the new Paisley Canal route, as well as Glasgow–Edinburgh via Shotts. Later in the decade, Glasgow City Council revealed their own plans for new stations, including some which had been talked about for decades but had never materialised. Ibrox was one of the names mentioned, partly to relieve congestion from football crowds on the Glasgow Underground.

In 2005, SPT and the West of Scotland Transport Partnership unveiled their new transport strategy, which proposed various rail route enhancements over the next twenty years. It highlighted a lack of capacity at Central and Queen Street stations and along lines such as the WCML, Glasgow–Paisley and Glasgow–Whifflet, with plans for improvement within six to ten years. It mentioned a long-term aspiration to reopen the rest of the line to Kilmacolm. By now, it seemed just about every route closed since Beeching was being planned for reopening!

Reinstating the railway to the Lanarkshire town of Larkhall was not a pipe-dream scenario; plans had been afoot for this scheme back in the early 1990s, with

Even next to some of the most built-up areas on the Strathclyde network, there are spots of open countryside, and the Motherwell–Cumbernauld route is no exception. On a cold winter's afternoon, a Class 318 unit crosses Braidhurst Viaduct near Motherwell, with the peak-time 1542 Milngavie–Coatbridge Central service. (Author's collection)

work beginning to reinstate the 3-mile route from Haughhead Junction (on the Hamilton Circle) to Larkhall after the new millennium. The new station in the town would be built on the site of the old Larkhall Central, which was formerly part of a route that extended to Strathaven and Coalburn, closing in 1965.

Larkhall was the largest town in the Strathclyde area not connected to the rail network before the line opened to passengers once again on 12 December 2005, with intermediate stations at Merryton and Chatelherault. It would become a new extension of the Argyle line, with a half-hourly service running to and from Dalmuir. These additional trains resulted in a higher service frequency over the Argyle line.

The West Coast Route Modernisation Programme was announced after privatisation and the Virgin Group's acquisition of WCML passenger operations. This would see the entire Glasgow–London route upgraded over the next few years to make it suitable for Virgin's new Class 390 Pendolino tilting trains – the most extensive series of engineering works on the section of line north of the border since the electrification project in the early 1970s.

It took several years for the project to get seriously underway, not helped by the Hatfield disaster in 2000 and the subsequent demise of Railtrack, to be replaced by Network Rail. Inevitably, the overall costs spiralled as delays mounted, and it was subsequently announced that the much talked-about plans to have Pendolinos running at 140mph would not come to fruition. In the end, they would only reach speeds of 125mph.

Upgrades to the Scottish section of the WCML would largely be left to the latter stages of the project in 2004–08, by which time Virgin 'Voyager' Class 220 and 'Super Voyager' Class 221 DEMUs had already taken over cross-country diagrams from Class 86s and HSTs. Their full introduction in 2002 was controversial, with serious overcrowding problems encountered on services right from the outset. Passengers were also irked by the peculiar, cramped seating arrangements and noise and vibrations from the underfloor engines. Virgin had gone one step forward only to take two steps back, with long-distance services to far-away destinations such as Penzance going from seven-coach HSTs and loco-hauled rakes to four-car Voyagers.

The decision to have shorter trains was expected to be outweighed by having a more frequent service, part of Virgin's new 'Operation Princess' timetable, which failed dismally. Rather embarrassingly, it resulted in HSTs being kept in service with Virgin CrossCountry for longer than expected into 2003 and even hired in from other operators after that. Longer trains and a more adequate timetable (which resulted in improved punctuality) were later implemented to improve this situation.

Pendolinos on the other hand were gradually put into service on the Glasgow Central–London Euston circuit from early 2004 and by the latter part of the year they had fully replaced trains hauled by classes 87 and 90. Their introduction was far more successful than that of the Voyagers and resulted in much shorter overall journey times by the time the bulk of the upgrade work on the WCML had been completed. Late winter and spring of 2004 had seen the first series of regular engineering works on the Glasgow–Carlisle section of the WCML in anticipation of this, with the line closed over selected weekends and some daytime services diverted without considerable delay over the GSWR main line via Kilmarnock and Dumfries. More planned diversions and bus replacement services continued over the next couple of years.

Introduction of a full 125mph timetable to the WCML in 2009 saw most journey times between Euston and Glasgow cut down to around four hours and thirty minutes in each direction. The fastest time is now four hours and eight minutes on the 1630 Euston–Glasgow service. The fastest journey from the summer 2003 timetable using Class 87/90-hauled trains was the 1030 ex-Euston (formerly the down Royal Scot), clocking in at five hours and five minutes (though this included additional stops at Oxenholme and Carlisle). This gave a saving of fifty-seven minutes with the Pendolinos.

A high-speed rail link to Glasgow Airport had been in the pipeline for some time, possibly as a light rail project. Located almost 7 miles from Glasgow city

High-rise flats tower above Kennishead station, on the Glasgow–Kilmarnock main line. (Author's collection)

centre near Paisley, the airport had always been rather cut off from the city, especially with no rail connection. The Scottish Executive concluded that this was unacceptable in the modern age and authorised the long-awaited Glasgow Airport Rail Link project on 29 November 2006. This would involve upgrading the 5.4-mile section of line from Shields Junction to Paisley Gilmour Street and adding a 1.2-mile branch line from near Paisley St James station to reach the airport.

Cancellation of the project after it had begun (due to government spending cuts), as announced on 17 September 2009, has passed into folklore. Since 2006, over £40 million of taxpayers' money is believed to have been put into the link, work which included adding two new platforms at Glasgow Central. This itself was fully completed and has since at least benefited the existing rail network, though it was initially proposed to allow for a fifteen-minute frequency of trains to the airport. If completed on schedule, the rail link would have been ready in plenty of time for the 2014 Commonwealth Games in the city. Its failure to materialise meant passengers had to continue to use a connecting bus service from Paisley Gilmour Street to the airport, with through rail–bus tickets available. The project's collapse attracted great criticism from all quarters, though it is a mystery why a link had not been built years earlier.

Upgrades to the Glasgow–Paisley main line still went ahead regardless after the airport project was cancelled, as part of Network Rail's £170 million Paisley Corridor Improvements (PCI) project. Decades after being reduced from a four-track to two-track section, operational capacity was being stretched, with increased train frequency during the intervening years. This included a revival in freight traffic, with a steady procession of coal trains to and from the Ayrshire coast now using the line throughout the day.

It was made possible to relay one of the old fast lines between Shields Junction and Paisley. A new third centre road was opened – fully electrified – early in 2012. Resignalling work also took place, primarily during a full-line closure over the 2011 Glasgow Fair weekend.

The PCI project was also complemented by a £9 million complete refurbishment of Paisley Gilmour Street station. This involved building a new extended overall roof with lattice girders in keeping with its original architecture. Formerly rather dark and dingy in appearance, the new-look Gilmour Street was fully revealed late in 2011, looking far brighter thanks to the light-painted furnishings and glazed roof. Nearby Paisley St James, which lies further away from Paisley town centre, was one in the list of stations suggested for closure in Transport Scotland's notorious Rail 2014 consultation the following year but was subsequently reprieved. On the Paisley Canal line, Mosspark was listed, along with Kennishead and Nitshill on the Glasgow–Kilmarnock route, plus Airbles near Motherwell.

The refurbished Paisley Gilmour Street station, another great example set by ScotRail in recent years. On 8 August 2013, Class 380 No. 380110 disembarks passengers at platform 4 on the 1528 Glasgow Central–Ardrossan Harbour, while 380116 waits with the 1453 Irvine–Glasgow. Platforms 1 and 2 off to the right serve the Inverclyde lines. (Author's collection)

The long-considered electrification of the Paisley Canal route took place in 2012, and 10 December that year saw Class 314 and 380 units take over all workings from Glasgow Central. The line had previously been electrified between Shields Junction and Corkerhill only, for EMU access to Corkerhill depot. ScotRail also have plans in the near future to finally electrify the Glasgow–East Kilbride/Kilmarnock and Edinburgh via Shotts lines, meaning that before long, diesel traction is sure to be in the minority within the city.

3

East End

The eastern side of Glasgow was traditionally always served by an east–west suburban train service via the city centre, which continues to this day. The ex-North British line via Glasgow Queen Street low-level extended to Edinburgh via Airdrie and Bathgate. The other line, operated by the Caledonian Railway via Central low-level and Bridgeton Cross, was of course the rival route. The Central line still continued to tunnel underground east from the city centre all the way out to Dalmarnock and Parkhead. However, the Queen Street line was only truly 'low-level' through the city centre, entering the open air at High Street station.

The line we know today as the City Union line across the Clyde through the Gorbals is so called as it was originally operated jointly by the Glasgow and South Western and the Edinburgh and Glasgow railway companies (latterly it was the GSWR and North British). It provided a link between lines at the north and south sides of the city and was also linked to the NBR low-level line. Completing the picture of the east side's network, the Motherwell–Cumbernauld line via Coatbridge was also formerly CR metals. This route connected the WCML to the Stirling–Perth main line at Greenhill Junction and was formerly used by Anglo-Scottish expresses to Perth and Inverness.

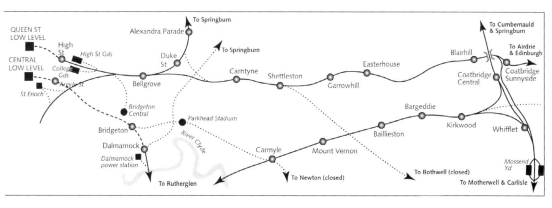

Passenger services between Glasgow and Edinburgh via Airdrie and Bathgate ceased in January 1956, though the line remained open for freight. Airdrie therefore became the eastern extent of the passenger network over the Queen Street low-level line and also the farthest point of 'Blue Train' operations when that route was electrified in 1960 and became the North Clyde line. Following that, the October 1964 closure of the Central low-level line would leave several key areas in the east end without stations.

Most notably there was no longer a nearby station to serve the Trongate and Merchant City areas after Glasgow Cross was shut. Further along the line, the loss of Parkhead Stadium station meant poorer transport links to Celtic FC's football ground. This part of town had already suffered badly before Beeching, with Gallowgate station on the City Union line disappearing before the Second World War, followed by Glasgow Green on the Central low-level line in 1953. Parkhead North station on the Airdrie line had closed in 1955.

The closure of the ex-CR low-level line meant the closure of Bridgeton Cross station, while Bridgeton Central survived as a terminus on a spur off the North Clyde route. Both eastern extensions of the 'Caley' route from Bridgeton–Rutherglen and Bridgeton–Carmyle would also shut. A British Steel factory kept the Carmyle–Newton section open for freight until the 1980s, while another spur which ran from Westburn Junction (near Carmyle) to Kirkhill closed in 1966. The Rutherglen–Airdrie East line was cut back to Whifflet Junction, Coatbridge, and remained open for freight. Completing the Beeching closures were the freight-only lines from Shettleston–Bothwell and Balornock–London Road goods yard.

The east end had arguably suffered more than any other part of the city under Beeching, and increasing social deprivation over the coming decades was not helped by the now meagre transport connections. The local authorities were already making plans back in the late 1960s to reopen the Central low-level route as a new electrified line, as published in the Greater Glasgow Transportation Survey's first report. Here there was mention made of installing a new junction at Bridgeton which would connect with the North Clyde route. Along with the plan to reintroduce passenger services on the Shields Junction–Bellgrove City Union line, known as the St John's Link, this was in essence an early version of the much discussed Glasgow Crossrail scheme, which has remained under consideration in recent years.

Subsequent plans were made for new stations at Glassford Street and Trongate (on the St John's Link), as well as the reopening of Bridgeton Cross. There were also new stations pencilled in at Provanmill and Alexandra East on the 'Garngad chord' which was to link the North Clyde and Springburn–Cumbernauld routes. Furthermore, there was a *second* chord planned between the Central and Queen Street lines, with a new Parkhead station along the way, creating a south-to-east

Bridgeton Central station is seen on 22 October 1979 – two weeks before it closed – with 303066 arriving under an interesting array of semaphore signals. The terminus remained in use for several years after closure to service EMUs such as this Class 303. (Tom Noble)

connection, while that at Bridgeton would allow a south-to-west link. Add all of this up and it made for one very extensive and costly line-construction plan.

East enders got something of a raw deal in the end, with the Central low-level line reopening, but only from Stobcross to Rutherglen, and no Garngad or Parkhead chords. Stations at Glassford Street and Trongate would also not materialise, though there was a new station built at Argyle Street, which would serve a busy shopping district of the city. Passengers using it today will notice that they descend below street level on a long escalator only to climb up again to reach the rather narrow, underground island platform. A lack of space due to the surrounding buildings necessitated this approach.

The new low-level Argyle line was officially inaugurated by Her Majesty the Queen on 1 November 1979, at the same time as the refurbished Glasgow Underground. Services began four days later using new thyristor-controlled Class 314 EMUs and this also saw the launch of the Greater Glasgow Trans-Clyde brand. The Trans-Clyde banner included buses and was created by the PTE with the objective of running a more integrated transport system in the city; at the same time, new bus services were created which connected with the trains, and through-tickets allowed seamless transfers between the two modes of transport. The tickets included various new types of travel pass and season tickets. New bus stations were also built at Anderston and Killermont Street. The latter of these – Buchanan Bus Station – was situated adjacent to the site of Buchanan Street railway station and is now the largest bus terminal in Scotland.

The new Argyle line brought with it the welcome reopening of stations at Dalmarnock and Bridgeton Cross. However, the latter became simply Bridgeton, as Bridgeton Central was closed at the same time, deemed to be no longer required. Despite this, the old terminus did remain in use as an EMU maintenance facility right up until the opening of Yoker depot in 1987. Meanwhile, at Rutherglen station, the Argyle line would once again join the West Coast Main Line and a new island platform was built next to the junction to serve the new trains. This resulted in the old platforms on the main line falling out of use.

Glasgow lost one of its four main lines to Edinburgh back in 1982, when the freight-only section of track between Airdrie and Bathgate was lifted. Seven years later in May 1989, the remaining line from Glasgow to Airdrie was extended east by 1½ miles to Drumgelloch, a new single-platform terminus built to serve the eastern side of Airdrie. Some Helensburgh/Balloch/Dalmuir–Airdrie services would now be extended through to Drumgelloch. The scheme to build the new station had been proposed back in the 1970s, but no thought had then been given to extending services any further east of there.

The Bellgrove accident earlier that year, on 6 March 1989, should have been a wake-up call to BR regarding single-lead junctions. One passenger and a driver were killed and fifty-four others were injured when the 1220 Milngavie–Springburn service collided head-on with the 1239 Springburn–Milngavie just to the east of Bellgrove Junction on the line via Duke Street. The Springburn-bound train had passed a signal at danger, resulting in it running on to the wrong line and straight into the path of the Milngavie service. Following the crash, one passenger and the driver of the Springburn train were subsequently trapped in the wreckage for over four hours before the rescue services managed to free them. This had proved very difficult due to the colossal impact of the collision, which had left one of the Class 303 EMU trailers tilted 12ft into the air at one end.

It was clear that a head-on collision of this nature could have been avoided with a double-lead junction arrangement. Yet the single-lead approach has remained at Bellgrove ever since. There was, however, a special SPAD (signal passed at danger) indicator signal put in place after the accident, to serve as an extra warning for trains approaching the junction from the west.

Glasgow was starting to enjoy an economic and cultural revival from the mid 1980s onwards, and Strathclyde PTE's investment in new rolling stock and route enhancements was very much part of this. The October 1993 reintroduction of passenger services on the Rutherglen–Coatbridge line, with a new half-hourly service from Glasgow Central high-level to Whifflet, opened up much-needed transport links to the city centre from a number of eastern residential areas. New stations on the line opened at Carmyle, Mount Vernon, Baillieston, Bargeddie, Kirkwood and Whifflet; all with twin platforms and 'bus shelter' waiting rooms. BR had also given consideration to reopening the line as an electrified route, but decided that could wait.

Privatisation brought a welcome freight boom to the Whifflet line and the adjoining Motherwell–Cumbernauld route, especially with imported coal from Ayrshire. Mossend Yard continued to be the main hub in the area, while the Freightliner container terminal at Gartsherrie, Coatbridge, handled several departures a day. August 1981 had seen the main line through Coatbridge Central electrified from Gartsherrie to Motherwell, allowing access to Mossend and Coatbridge yards for classes 86 and 87 among others.

While the volume of freight had expanded on this route, passenger traffic had declined. Anglo-Scottish services, such as the Inverness–Euston 'Clansman', had ceased or taken to running via Edinbugh, meaning that the Coatbridge Central–Gartsherrie section was now freight-only. That was until 1997, when ScotRail inaugurated a new hourly shuttle service from Motherwell to Cumbernauld, using heritage Class 101 DMUs, which were later replaced

Passenger services returned to the Rutherglen–Whifflet line in 1993 after being lost to Beeching in the 1960s. The reopened Baillieston station, seen here, received a modern style of footbridge which has additional ramps for disabled access. Sprinter 156449 pauses on 18 January 2014, with the 1316 Glasgow Central–Whifflet. (Author's collection)

by Class 156s and 158s. Services would call at Whifflet, Coatbridge Central and Greenfaulds.

Big changes were on the horizon in the east end of Glasgow after the new millennium. The biggest would be the rebuilding of the Glasgow–Edinburgh line via Airdrie and Bathgate, seemingly off the agenda back in 1989 when the closed route was resurrected as far as Drumgelloch only. Although there had been a number of line reinstatements in Strathclyde since Beeching, this would only be the second true main line reopening and the first since the Argyle line in 1979. It would provide a fourth rail link from Glasgow to Edinburgh – with four trains an hour – and open up through-journeys to the Scottish capital from Helensburgh, Dumbarton and various suburbs in Glasgow's west and east ends, which had previously necessitated passengers travelling into the city centre to change trains.

Work on the Airdrie–Bathgate rail link was very extensive and began in late 2006. The line would be electrified and double track the whole way, laid over the former trackbed, which had been converted into a cycle path since closure over twenty-five years before. The cycle path would be rerouted alongside the reinstated line, whilst Airdrie station would undergo a thorough refurbishment,

The 1037 Edinburgh Waverley–Milngavie trundles into High Street station in the rain on 18 January 2014, formed of two Class 334s, No. 334007 leading. The overgrown area alongside the retaining wall to the right used to be College goods yard, with High Street yard located on the opposite side. (Author's collection)

with a second through-platform being brought back into use. A modern footbridge would be built, incorporating elevators, as well as a 139-space car park. Drumgelloch – opened less than twenty years earlier – would close to be replaced by a new through-station with two platforms, just 550m to the east along the line.

The Airdrie–Bathgate link was completed on time and on budget, to the tune of £300 million funded by the Scottish Executive. The 15-mile-long route opened to traffic on 12 December 2010, amid one of the worst winters in Scotland for decades. The 'Big Freeze' had delayed the opening of new stations at Drumgelloch, Caldercruix and Armadale (these would open early the following year), whilst introduction of a full timetable also had to be postponed until the following May, due to the late introduction of new Class 380 EMUs (these would work the Inverclyde lines and in turn free up Class 334s for the Airdrie-Bathgate duties). The initial service from Glasgow to Edinburgh was hourly Monday–Friday and half-hourly at weekends.

When fully up and running, the proper timetable consisted of four trains per hour: two from Milngavie and two from Helensburgh to Edinburgh, with the latter journey taking just over two hours. Half-hourly Balloch–Airdrie workings also continued. The Airdrie–Bathgate section itself had not seen any scheduled passenger traffic for fifty-four years at the time of its reopening.

Since the Airdrie-Bathgate link, the overall picture has been good for the railway in Glasgow's east end. As the focal point for the 2014 Commonwealth Games, the area has seen mass land redevelopment and improved transport links. An extension of the M74 motorway, opened in 2011, now allows improved road access, but the railway has not been left behind; the Airdrie–Bathgate reopening is a firm assurance of this (incidentally this project did not run over-budget, unlike the new road).

Additional improvements include electrification of the Whifflet route, a line which was once considered to be the most unsafe in Britain, with record levels of vandalism and sabotage. It is in the process of going 'under the wires' at the time of writing, which would at least seem to safeguard passenger services that were previously lost to Beeching. The suggested closure and subsequent reprieve given to Duke Street station on the Springburn line in 2012 marked the only time anything remotely like the Beeching cuts has been threatened in the east end in recent years, an encouraging sign yet a reminder that stations still need the patronage if they are to remain open.

4

West End

The River Clyde had a lot to do with the coming of the railway in the western side of Glasgow. Flowing away from the city centre towards Clydebank, the revered shipyards of Yarrows and John Brown & Co. formerly dominated the northern banks of the river and produced a steady stream of goods traffic on the railway, with connecting lines along the docks. This was especially notable during the Second World War. The docks were also the birthplace of famous ocean liners such as RMS *Queen Mary* and *Queen Elizabeth*, as well as warships like HMS *Hood*.

As the river carried on west out to sea at Dumbarton, the railway followed it, right towards the pier at Craigendoran, where Clyde steamers connected with

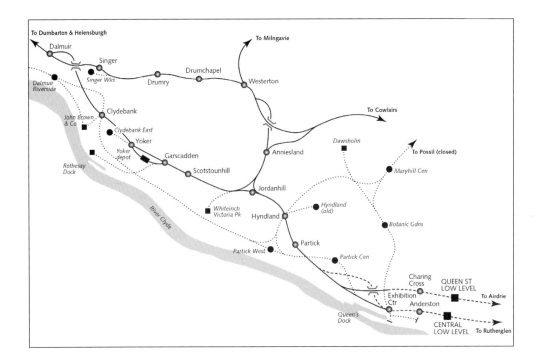

trains for cruises 'doon the watter'. This belonged to the North British Railway, whose city low-level route through Glasgow Queen Street divided into various connecting lines serving the suburbs that ultimately converged again at Dalmuir Park before heading along the scenic Clyde estuary.

Further west lay Helensburgh and the West Highland Line to Fort William and Mallaig. Passenger services from the Highlands shared the NBR's route through Drumchapel and Westerton with intensive local workings from Balloch, Helensburgh and Milngavie. There was also a station built to serve the large Singer sewing machine factory in Clydebank. Expansion of the works saw the line take a slight deviation for a few miles to the north in 1907, with a new Singer station (named after the complex) built in its place. In theory this should have spelt the end for the old station but it was subsequently retained on a short spur and became a private terminus known as Singer Works. Its six platforms were a hive of activity every day as a continuous stream of special workers' trains – not listed in the public timetable – served the factory well into the 1960s.

The North British, later LNER, had an alternative route through industrial Clydebank and Yoker which left the Drumchapel route at Dalmuir Park, essentially a long loop that rejoined it near Jordanhill. A short stub served Clydebank East, the original western terminus of this line, which was replaced by Clydebank Central through-station in 1897 but still retained. Heading east, the line weaved through the tenement-lined streets of Hyndland and Partick then traversed more docklands along the Clyde, before plunging underground near Charing Cross. Short branches served the termini of Hyndland and Whiteinch Victoria Park, the latter of which closed to passengers in 1951.

The Caledonian/LMS had a slightly more muted presence in the west end. Their Glasgow Central low-level route essentially skirted the North British line from Dumbarton, through Dalmuir Riverside, Yoker and Whiteinch, running close to the riverbank the whole way. It had branches connecting to most of the harbours and shipyards, such as Rothesay Dock and Yoker power station. Both the LMS and LNER had tramway branches in the area as well, joining the railway to the docks at Clydebank (John Brown & Co.), Scotstoun and Whiteinch.

A triangular junction surrounded the Caledonian's Partick West station, where the line towards Maryhill Central tunnelled northwards. For the most part, the line was subterranean, like the section through Glasgow city centre, but with a scenic open-air section near Maryhill where it wound past the River Kelvin on a steep retaining wall. Another triangular junction at Maryhill saw the northern line to Possil and Springburn diverge, with the other route heading below ground level once again to rejoin the Partick route at Stobcross.

The 'Caley' line all the way from Partick to Dalmarnock was expensive to build and renowned for both its dark, smoky environment and the utilitarian appearance of its stations. A prime example that can still be seen today is the derelict underground Botanic Gardens station, where the old platforms, tunnels and trackbed still survive intact. It closed in 1939, and the line in 1964, but the scene here still oozes with atmosphere.

1959 saw Clydebank East station closed in the run-up to electrification of what would become the North Clyde line; incorporating both the Yoker and Westerton routes into Dalmuir Park. The spur into Singer Works station was also electrified, while the upmarket residential area of Hyndland received a brand-new island platform through-station next to where the line crossed Clarence Drive, opened in November 1960. The old Hyndland terminus half a mile to the east was closed, though a new maintenance depot was built on the site to service the new 'Blue Trains', and so the short branch remained busy.

Beeching did not look favourably upon the west end's intricate rail network, especially with multiple stations essentially serving the same areas. Crow Road, near Hyndland, had closed back in 1960 for this very reason. It was therefore inevitable that the Central low-level line would succumb on 5 October 1964, with complete closure from Partick Central to Rutherglen and the remaining sections reduced to freight-only. Two years later, freight was also withdrawn

The remains of the approaches to Whiteinch Victoria Park station, which shut to passengers in 1951 and freight in 1965. The trackbed is now a nature trail. (Author's collection)

and the track lifted from Partick–Possil and Possil–Stobcross, while the branch to the Queen's Dock at Stobcross, accessed from the North Clyde line, shut in July 1968. Meanwhile, Whiteinch had lost its goods facilities in May 1965, but electrification works trains were regularly stabled there until the branch closed completely in February 1967.

Following Beeching's closures, a couple of station name-changes eventually followed, with Dalmuir Park changed to Dalmuir and Clydebank Central becoming simply Clydebank. The area saw the same pattern of industrial decline and the resultant reduction in freight traffic that was evident all over the city. A decline in fortunes of the sewing-machine factory saw the closure of Singer Works station in 1969, with the plant itself eventually falling in 1980.

Financial problems at the shipyards, rationalised to become Upper Clyde Shipbuilders, saw an infamous 'work-in' by their employees which ultimately saved the remaining yards, though rail traffic was doomed. The Partick Central–Yoker section of line was closed to freight traffic in October 1978, though a shipbreaker's yard and Chivas Brothers whisky plant at Dalmuir, together with a naval fuel depot in Old Kilpatrick, still provided traffic on the short remaining line which left the North Clyde route at Yoker.

On the passenger side, most of BR and GGPTE's 1970s line reinstatement plans were actually delivered in the west end, unlike in other parts of the city. A new line through Maryhill and Kelvindale, joining the North Clyde line at Hyndland, was one which would not materialise (until 2005, when the similar Maryhill–Anniesland section opened), but the reinstatement of the Central low-level route as the Argyle line marked a radical change to the public timetable. This would see the former Caledonian route through Anderston and Stobcross reach a new junction at Finnieston, where it would join the North Clyde line and continue over these metals the whole way out to Dalmuir. Services would be virtually doubled over the Partick–Jordanhill section, while Argyle line services would use both the Westerton and Yoker routes to Dalmuir. There was to be no reinstatement of the sections out to Possil, or the old approach out to Dalmuir via Clydebank Riverside.

Also central to both the Argyle line and Glasgow Underground reopenings (the latter was closed for refurbishment during 1977–80) was the building of a new interchange station at Partick, which was a first for the city as a whole. The upper platforms would serve the main railway and the lower ones the Subway, with a joint ticket office and bus station right outside to offer further connections. Partickhill station – the only mainline railway station in Partick to survive Beeching – would close, with its replacement opening only yards away at the opposite side of the Dumbarton Road underbridge, on 17 December 1979, twelve days after the Argyle line was reopened.

The Argyle line: A railway reborn

Just 4½ miles of the original Glasgow Central low-level line, from Stobcross–Rutherglen, was reopened in 1979, though the name 'Argyle line' was subsequently applied to the whole route from Dalmuir to Lanark. Beeching's closures had resulted in rail services in the city previously being split between one section north of the River Clyde and one to the south. The Argyle line would rejoin the two parts, as would the refurbished Glasgow Subway, with around £80 million being spent collectively to deliver both schemes.

Since its 1964 closure, the tunnels and trackbed of the low-level line had remained intact, mainly because there were always plans to reopen it. Nevertheless, significant repairs had to take place to bring it back into use, namely brickwork strengthening and drainage work. Furthermore, decades of steam operation had left a hefty covering of soot all along the tunnels and walls, which had to be removed with power hoses.

The biggest engineering feature on the reopened line was the burrowing junction built at Kelvinhaugh. Eastbound trains would leave the North Clyde line at Finnieston and then tunnel directly underneath it to reach the new Finnieston station. However, westbound trains took a different approach, joining the North Clyde at a separate junction slightly to the east.

Finnieston station was essentially a rebuild of the original platforms at Stobcross, but would be renamed Exhibition Centre in 1986 with the opening of the SECC arena. A new siding was built there in 1979 to allow trains to stable and turn back after terminating at Anderston, while Dalmuir received a new bay platform for the same purposes. Anderston station itself was an original, built by the Glasgow Central Railway in 1896 but reopened with the new line.

A noticeable feature of the reopened Argyle line was that the track was laid on a base of concrete slabs instead of ballast within the underground section from Stobcross to Dalmarnock. This allowed the trackbed to be of a reduced depth and thus gave adequate clearance for the overhead wires. It also meant the track was more suitable for running at higher speeds and much less maintenance was required, which was especially useful since permanent way teams had to work in pitch-black tunnels. A concrete trackbed is also found on the North Clyde line where it tunnels beneath the city centre.

The addition of the Argyle line and more connecting bus services in the Strathclyde network saw a notable increase in rail travel, even if it failed to match the figures anticipated by GGPTE. Drumchapel was one of the stations which benefited from new bus services, which continue to this day. Meanwhile, the last vestiges of freight from the Clyde shipyards would disappear in the 1980s, when traffic was withdrawn from the Old Kilpatrick fuel depot in 1986 and Arnott Young shipbreakers at Dalmuir the year after. The Rothesay Dock branch was reactivated for a brief period in 1988 for coal traffic to Kincardine power station, while whisky tankers were still conveyed from Keith to Dalmuir Riverside (via Mossend) into the Railfreight Distribution era of the early 1990s.

Nearby Singer had previously been the scene of a tragic accident, when the driver of a freight train died after being electrocuted by overhead wires. Danny Bradley of Eastfield depot was in charge of the 1258 Cadder Yard–Fort William working, which had been sent into the passing loop near the station. The train was conveying china clay in covered wagons, but one of the covers had blown loose in the wet and windy weather. After bringing the train to a halt, the driver was attempting to tie down the cover when it struck the electric catenary and killed him. The goods loop here was later removed on 2 July 1989, when Singer signal box closed.

There was another accident near here on 30 January 1987, involving EMU 303051, which was newly refurbished at Springburn works. Just after returning from the works, the empty unit ran away from Westerton and collided head-on with Class 37 No. 37011 a few miles down the line, but thankfully nobody was hurt. Both the 303 and the 37 were withdrawn from service as a result.

Dalmuir Riverside on 20 September 1984, with Eastfield Class 27 No. 27204 in charge of the 6N31 Speedlink trip to Mossend Yard. This train served the nearby Chivas Regal bottling plant, with the third and fourth wagons in the rake used to convey whisky from a distillery in Keith. (John Baker)

Glasgow Museum of Transport and Riverside Museum

Glasgow's first transport museum was established in 1964 at the former Coplawhill tram depot in Pollokshields, showcasing trams, buses and other historic vehicles. It moved home to the Kelvin Hall, Partick, in 1987 and became a very popular visitor attraction for many years. The railway presence there was dominated by four pre-grouping era steam locomotives on static display: Caledonian Railway 'Single' No. 123, Highland Railway 'Jones Goods' No. 103, Great North of Scotland Railway class 'F' No. 49 *Gordon Highlander* and North British Railway 'Glen' class No. 256 *Glen Douglas*. All four of them had previously been returned to steam by BR in the early 1960s, when they worked a number of special trains around the country. Glasgow and South Western Railway 0-6-0 tank No. 9 was also preserved in the Kelvin Hall.

In addition, there was a replica 1930s-era street scene in the museum, which led to a wonderfully recreated Glasgow Underground station, displaying preserved Glasgow District Subway cars. This was subsequently moved along with most other exhibits to the new Riverside Museum, which opened nearby in 2011 to replace the Kelvin Hall venue.

The Riverside Museum has the addition of a Glasgow-built South African Railways 4-8-2 steam locomotive on display. Meanwhile, *Glen Douglas* was relocated here after several years on loan to the Scottish Railway Exhibition in Bo'ness, swapping places with *Gordon Highlander*.

The new museum is located on the banks of the River Clyde at Pointhouse Quay, in the redeveloped Glasgow Harbour district near Partick. Entry is free and it is well worth a visit for transport aficionados.

HR 'Jones Goods' No. 103 and GNSR No. 49 *Gordon Highlander* preserved in the old Museum of Transport, in the Kelvin Hall. (Author's collection)

Dalmuir station became a significant hub for Strathclyde PTE operations after becoming the end point of the Argyle line. It also became a booked stop for West Highland Line services from the late 1980s and got its own through-train to London courtesy of the Fort William sleeper! The establishment of a train crew depot was somewhat rudimentary though, using portakabins stacked on the platforms that were not replaced until a proper building was constructed in 2012.

Vandalism also became notorious at Dalmuir over the years, with a tall fence having to be built around the roofs of the adjacent high flats to prevent missiles being thrown on to the track. A British Transport Police office was also eventually built at the station, which, along with improved CCTV, has created a safer environment for passengers.

Few can be prepared, however, for the effects of extreme weather conditions on the railway; 1994 especially springs to mind, when rainstorms and flooding over the weekend of 10–11 December saw the River Kelvin burst its banks and water tumble into the underground section of the Argyle line. More than 110,000 tonnes of debris and water covered the line between Exhibition Centre and Argyle Street, trapping two eastbound Class 314 units at Glasgow Central low-level in the process. At both this location and Argyle Street, the water was more than 3m deep and came close to submerging the train. Rainfall that weekend

On 23 January 2013, Saltire-liveried 320302 leaves Anniesland with the 1107 Larkhall–Dalmuir, while a First ScotRail Class 158 stands in the bay platform with the 1151 to Glasgow Queen Street via Maryhill. (Author's collection)

had been the heaviest ever recorded in the Strathclyde area and it also caused disruption to the Subway network.

The Argyle line would end up closed for more than nine months for repairs to be carried out, which eventually cost Railtrack around £3 million. Engineers had a real job on their hands; having firstly to pump out all of the water and then to begin to rebuild most of the stonework, track, signalling and electrics. The line finally reopened on 24 September 1995 with a special ceremony.

Privatisation brought fresh investment by ScotRail and SPT in many of the west end's stations, with particular attention paid to improving road–rail connections and disabled access. A major project was an extensive multi-million-pound rebuilding of 1979-built Partick, which commenced in late 2005 and was ongoing for several years while the station stayed open to the public. The original entrance to the station and ticket office area for both the low-level trains and Underground was replaced with a much larger, extended main building, incorporating a glass frontage.

The new facilities at Partick fully opened on 31 March 2009. Much larger waiting rooms replaced the old ones on both platforms, now accessible via stairs and lifts in addition to the main escalators, which eased overcrowding during rush hours. New digital departure boards, a WHSmith newsagents, coffee stand and extra side-entrance were other key additions. There were also great improvements to the surrounding roads around the same time, but the station still currently lacks its own car park, the adjacent Morrisons supermarket providing the nearest equivalent.

Overall, Partick now has a station much more suitable for its level of custom. It has long been busy with commuters, but patronage increased tenfold after the opening of the Larkhall route in 2005, then the new buildings and Airdrie–Bathgate

The new state-of-the-art concourse of Partick station. The stairs ahead lead to the main line platforms while the Subway entrance is out of shot to the left. (Author's collection)

route a few years later. Usage has also virtually doubled in the past decade. As a result, Partick is currently the busiest double track station in Scotland and sixth busiest station in the country overall, with fourteen trains each way per hour Monday–Saturday, plus more at peak times. The section from there to Jordanhill represents one of the busiest main lines in Britain, with capacity now fully stretched.

Other stations receiving improvements in recent years have included Dalmuir and Hyndland, which both got new footbridges incorporating lifts in 2010 and 2012 respectively. Hyndland also now benefits from an automatic vending machine in common with other stations in the west end such as Charing Cross and Westerton, though Westerton, Bearsden, Drumchapel and Dalmuir are the only ones to have extensive car parks. Meanwhile, automatic ticket barriers have appeared at Charing Cross and Anderston, and Exhibition Centre now provides good access not only to the SECC, but also to the Clyde Auditorium and Hydro arena.

Post-millennium, the North Clyde and Argyle lines that make up most of Glasgow's west end rail network have benefited greatly from a massive upsurge in city commuter travel, which goes to show that for speed and convenience, there really is no substitute for rail. The fast and intensive electric services of the present day allow plenty of options for travellers, and the additional traffic from the Larkhall and Airdrie–Bathgate routes has been another welcome boost in this respect. Throw in the Subway trains and a regular, if somewhat unreliable, bus service too, and it is fair to say that west enders must be very satisfied with their transport links.

5

Termini

Glasgow Queen Street

The smaller of Glasgow's two remaining major terminus stations today, Glasgow Queen Street could well be regarded as a scaled-down version of its big brother down by the Clyde. Still devoid of overhead wires – at least until the Edinburgh and Glasgow main line is electrified in the near future – Queen Street has changed relatively little over the years, partly due to its location in a deep cutting half-below street level which allows little expansion. It remains a hive of activity today, with 20.9 million passengers per year (57,000 per day) according to the latest statistics, making it the third busiest station in Scotland and fifth busiest in the UK outside London.

A view under the trainshed at Queen Street on 13 June 2007, with Class 170 Turbostars displaying a multitude of liveries. (Author's collection)

Train movements at this north-facing terminus are almost as frequent as at Central, restricted due to the fact that there are only two approach lines into the station. The Cowlairs Incline carries the railway uphill through the 1,040yd-long Cowlairs Tunnel, on a formidable gradient of between 1 in 41 and 1 in 51, which begins immediately at the platform ends. In the days of steam, this necessitated the use of banking locomotives to assist northbound trains out of the station. Prior to 1908, trains were actually hauled up the bank by rope, which was powered by a stationary steam engine. This was abolished in 1908 after what was almost a serious accident a few years earlier.

Queen Street was opened on 21 February 1842 by the Edinburgh & Glasgow Railway with a tightly spaced six-platform layout. Originally, Cowlairs Tunnel was longer and extended as far forward as the Cathedral Street bridge over the station. However, the North British Railway took control of Queen Street in 1865 and later opened up part of the tunnel and extended the platforms, allowing much more daylight into the scene. They also added the large, overall glass roof which is seen today. This elegant structure was the work of North British Railway engineer James Carswell and is 450ft long, with a central arch spanning 170ft and reaching a maximum height of 79ft off the ground.

Throughout its lifetime under the LNER and British Railways, platform space at Queen Street remained at a premium. At best, there were nine platforms before the neighbouring Buchanan Street terminus shut in November 1966 and its traffic was transferred there. The resultant extra trains would result in major modernisation work taking place over the next few years. Despite the increase, the nine platforms would be reduced to seven, through Queen Street losing a few of its own services (such as to Kirkintilloch), which had freed up a certain amount of capacity. January 1964 had seen the closure of the former goods depot at the east end of the station next to North Hanover Street and this would be converted into a car park and taxi rank.

The biggest change to occur along with platform alterations was the remodelling of trackwork and signalling in 1967. The original signal box which spanned the tunnel mouth was demolished and all semaphore signals were replaced with colour lights, allowing a half-minute frequency of train movements. Control was transferred to Cowlairs signal box at the top of the bank, with track circuits also brought into use.

There were big changes on the Queen Street concourse as well, following Beeching. This area was eventually enlarged, with a new left luggage facility and refurbishment of the cafeteria and bar. A mail and parcels office still remained, courtesy of BR's Red Star service, which used passenger trains to transport packages around the country. Meanwhile, an entire new travel centre/ticket office was constructed at the west side of the station, along with a new staff headquarters and operations centre alongside platform 2. This resulted in the demolition of the iconic arches at the Dundas Street entrance, where an additional entrance to the refurbished Buchanan Street Subway station was later added in 1979.

Through the years, not only did Queen Street's bottleneck approach lines through Cowlairs Tunnel have to cope with a constant stream of passenger trains arriving and departing; there was also a steady flow of empty coaching stock and light engine movements (to and from Eastfield depot) right up until the end of regular loco-haulage in 1990. From the 1980s onwards, a Class 26 diesel would usually be employed as the station pilot to handle the ECS workings to and from Cowlairs carriage sidings. Train lengths could still pose problems at the short platforms and it was for this reason that Edinburgh–Glasgow services were

Lunchtimes at Queen Street Station: 1988

On 28 February 1988, Class 37 No. 37409 *Loch Awe* begins its 102-mile journey west with the 1220 service to Oban. (David Webster)

Hybrid DMU sets were also common at the terminus. Plain blue-liveried Class 104 No. 104458 has been made into a three-car formation with a blue and grey 101 centre car, seen on 4 August. (David Webster)

A visit on 13 September sees the station pilot, Railfreight Class 26 No. 26037, backing on to an Edinburgh push–pull rake for a trip up to Cowlairs carriage sidings. (David Webster)

With plenty of excess 'clag', 47577 makes a rousing departure on the 1333 to Inverness on 27 September. The 47 carries an unusual version of 'Large Logo' livery, lacking the extended yellow cabsides. (David Webster)

restricted to a maximum of six coaches. A summer service to Inverness, Oban or Fort William could load up to seven or eight, but nothing more.

The atmosphere around Queen Street has changed considerably through the years. The heavy chatter of diesel locomotive exhausts has been replaced by the constant whir of modern DMU engines, with loco-hauled trains now very rare. Once a very gloomy place, the station has a far brighter environment thanks to additional roof glass and the white marble platform tiles added in recent years, though the construction of Buchanan Galleries shopping centre over the tunnel

Queen Street Low-Level

Glasgow Queen Street's low-level station was opened in 1886 and assumed responsibility for some of the local services to free up space at the high-level. It was built at a right angle to the main station and directly underneath it, being bordered at either end by lengthy tunnels and totally underground save for a short open-air section at each side to allow some daylight. Here there were also two signal boxes positioned on gantries above the track to control movements through the four platforms.

The low level was refurbished and resignalled with colour lights as 'Blue Trains' replaced Class V1 and V3 2-6-2 tanks on North Clyde suburban services. The station was also reduced to just two running lines, with the central island platform taken out of use, though it is still in place today. The two platforms in use nowadays are numbered 8 and 9 (in accordance with platforms 1–7 on the high-level).

Another refurbishment of the platforms followed in the 1980s, hence the yellow plastic walls and seating in place today – very 1980s! BR proposed installing escalators in the 1990s to replace the entrance stairs but never got round to it, though lifts eventually appeared instead. Today, there are two entrances to the platforms – at Dundas Street and North Hanover Street – and until fairly recently there was also a small newsagent's kiosk located on platform 8.

Saturday shoppers board at Queen Street low-level. (Author's collection)

entrance in 1999 did entomb the station slightly again. Bright LED departure screens have replaced the older dot-matrix versions, which in turn had replaced the original manual boards, while automatic ticket barriers complete the picture of modernisation.

There are still three entrances to the main Queen Street high level station: the principal one on Dundas Street, and the others on North Hanover and West George Streets. One relic of the past is the Millennium Hotel overlooking George Square, which was formerly the North British Hotel. Until the 1980s it was railway property and had been extended over part of the station area during the previous decade.

Major changes are also planned for Queen Street as part of the Edinburgh to Glasgow Improvement Programme (EGIP). The age-old problem of short platforms will be addressed by extending the running lines further down towards the concourse. The concourse will therefore be pushed back, but extended around a new glass frontage over the George Square entrance.

Glasgow Central

In Central station, the city of Glasgow has one grand terminus that certainly rivals the King's Crosses and Eustons of this world. Architecturally, it still boasts traditional Victorian furnishings all around, dominated by a magnificent ridged glass roof that is the largest anywhere in the world. The whole station covers over 2sq. miles and is currently the busiest in Scotland and busiest in the UK outside London, with more than 35 million people a year using it (only around 80 per cent of these are believed to be passengers). As such, Central's wide and airy concourse is very much the epitome of life in Glasgow, including its ever-present feral pigeon population!

Central's seemingly beautifully formed roof of today is actually a composite of three different parts; the first being built when the station was first opened by the Caledonian Railway on 1 August 1879. The terminus replaced an original one at Bridge Street on the south side of the River Clyde, after the 'Caley' gained running powers to build a new bridge across the water. However, Central's eight platforms, stretching on to a main entrance on Gordon Street with the adjoining Central Hotel, were soon deemed insufficient for the growing volume of traffic. An initial expansion to nine platforms, plus widening of the approach bridge across Argyle Street, was not enough and in 1901 a major rebuild began.

The rebuild is where the other parts of the roof come in. The initial section across the main concourse had extensions added to cover what was now thirteen platforms, which were lengthened, stretching the station right over the Argyle Street bridge. The extended covered areas can be recognised today by their

Class 108 DMU No. 108340 – with a Class 101 centre car – leaves Glasgow Central on the 1315 to Barrhead, on 22 September 1988. (David Webster)

different style of glass panels and arches, supported by curved trusses, while the original ones over the concourse are straight. Platforms 9–13 were also longer and converged on a new bridge over the Clyde (752ft long, with eight tracks) added alongside the original structure (which had four tracks). Furthermore, the extension of the station across the Argyle Street bridge created what became known as the 'Hielanman's Umbrella', which was soon filled with shops as well as giving Glaswegians shelter from the storm.

There would be no vast changes again at Central until the late 1950s, when major resignalling and track rationalisation began in the run-up to electrification. The year 1961 would see the original bridge over the Clyde removed and all of the 1,000 trains a day at the station concentrated on the wider, newer structure. (The old bridge's piers, however, still stand to this day.) The alternative of rebuilding the dilapidated old bridge was ruled out due to high costs.

A new Glasgow Central Signalling Centre was built at Bridge Street Junction to replace the original box alongside the bridge, with colour light signals replacing the semaphores. From June 1966, it would start handling the additional traffic gained from the closed Glasgow St Enoch station. Thus, similarly to Queen Street terminus, Central would actually gain from the effects of the Beeching cuts.

The 1970s still saw a plethora of diesel traction at Central, even after the electrification of the West Coast Main Line. Most of this was in the form of DMUs, on the ex-GSWR routes formerly served by St Enoch. With the station operating at full capacity, departures were virtually by the minute, sometimes even more frequent. Classes 20, 25 and 27 were all used as station pilots, usually manned by Polmadie drivers, and they certainly had their work cut out: working continuous empty coaching stock moves throughout the day to and from the carriage sidings at Larkfield, Smithy Lye and Bellahouston, though latterly these workings were handled more by the train engines rather than the pilots.

Many old traditions from the steam era still survived at Central after Beeching. Into the 1970s there were still regular summer holiday extras to and from destinations all over the country, with the Glasgow Fair fortnight in July being especially busy. A great number of special arrangements had to be made for this period, including extra staffing and plans for crowd control with passengers directed to separate queues for each respective destination.

A look at the 1970 Glasgow Fair weekend of 17–20 July reveals a ban on all first-class travel bookings on Ayrshire services on the Monday. As well as relief workings to Ayrshire coast destinations such as Largs, Ardrossan, Ayr and Girvan, there were specials running to locations in England, such as Blackpool, Sheffield and Manchester. Some of these were overnight trains and many used the GSWR main line as well as the WCML. An additional pilot locomotive was also provided at Central for the extra ECS workings.

The additional Fair traffic gradually dwindled through the years as holidaymakers started to prefer going abroad or moved towards road transport. Football specials also became less of a feature, though matches at Hampden Park today can still produce a few extras, albeit using EMUs instead of loco-haulage. Special queuing arrangements are also made for this purpose.

Central would go on to benefit from a few more refurbishment programmes through the years. The first during the 1980s saw the station brightened up somewhat, similarly to Queen Street, with light-coloured floor tiles now covering the main concourse. Another major change was the provision of a new large dot-matrix departure board in the same area, replacing the manually operated boards. A smaller version was also helpfully provided nearer to the entrance of Central low-level station. Red Star parcels facilities also opened there in 1986, in addition to the Royal Mail travelling post office trains which continued to work out of the terminus.

A further upgrade to the station was due again in the late 1990s and this included reglazing the entire roof – 6.8 acres (48,000 individual panes) of glass in total. Shops – both in the station confines and under the 'Hielanman's Umbrella' – had

'No heat' Class 37 No. 37373 leaves Central on 7 September 1988, standing in for the booked Class 47 on the 1333 to Carlisle via Dumfries. The 37/3 sub-class was dedicated to coal and iron ore traffic out of Ravenscraig steelworks at this time, and to find one on a passenger train was very rare indeed. (David Webster)

their exteriors restored to a Victorian style, while the Umbrella had the station name applied in large gold lettering at each end. The stone archway between platforms 11 and 12 was also adorned with this proud legend. The improvements were carried out by Railtrack, since succeeded by Network Rail, who now own Glasgow Central as well as a number of other large stations in the UK (hence the different style of signage). Queen Street, on the other hand, is the property of ScotRail, the only company that operates there.

After this refurbishment, Central was very much a station befitting the twenty-first century. But the work didn't stop there; 2005 saw the latest LED departure boards replace the 1980s dot-matrix versions, and then 2009 saw work begin on building the two new platforms to serve the Glasgow Airport Rail Link, which still continued after the airport plan was shelved. The short platform 11A near the bridge (once called West Bank Siding), which had been used invariably for stabling light engines or units and parcels traffic through the years, was removed and two new lines were laid between platforms 10 and 11, running under the conveniently spaced entrance archway. The inner station car park there had to be removed to accommodate the new, short platforms, which were numbered 12 and 13, opening in May 2010. The old platforms 12 and 13 became 14 and 15.

Evening rush hour at Central. (Author's collection)

One of the few changes at Central since then has been the addition of automatic ticket barriers at all platforms, bar numbers 1 and 2. The first two platforms are still the main ones used for the London expresses, being one of the key traditions that has survived at the station throughout the years, even if the trains are no longer hauled by locomotives or carry the fabled carriage-side nameboards of the Royal Scot or Mid-Day Scot. The growing monopoly of multiple units has also ended the once familiar sight of electric locomotives stabled in the sidings to the south of the Clyde bridge. Across from there, the massive power signal box (Glasgow Central Signalling Centre) has also been taken out of use, with December 2008 seeing control of the station transferred to the West of Scotland Signalling Centre at Cowlairs.

Continued tender loving care in recent years has ensured that Central station continues to be a great advert for the city of Glasgow and its rail system. As part of the 2014 Commonwealth Games preparations, it will undoubtedly be a real centre of attention, and this paved the way for a £250,000 project that saw its roof cleaned from top to bottom. Now ready for one of the biggest years in its history, there has never been a better time to view operations at this 135-year-old terminus.

Glasgow Central Low-Level

In the grand setting of Central station, it is easy to forget that it also has its own underground platforms serving the electrified Argyle line. Despite playing second fiddle to the main terminus, the low-level platforms 16 and 17 have been a constant feature there since 1896, save for the period 1964–79 when the Argyle line was closed.

Unlike the high-level, the low-level station has a very austere appearance, with the single island platform still clad in the same bricked surface present since reopening in 1979. As in steam days, there are no ventilation shafts so there is subsequently no daylight. There was another island platform prior to the station being rebuilt in the 1970s.

The low-level station is well-used given its city centre location and connections to the main platforms up the stairs. Rush hours are particularly busy. In addition to the electric service – usually six trains per hour each way – railtours and freight traffic can occasionally be diverted this way too, with the result that many diesel classes have made surprise appearances in recent years.

The dark cavern of Central low-level station, with 320316 handling a Larkhall working. Class 320s were not seen here regularly until 2011, when a mass reshuffle of diagrams saw many of them transferred on to Argyle line duties. (Author's collection)

6

Diesel Traction

Shunting locomotives

The longest-serving class of diesel in the Glasgow area is undoubtedly the Class 08 350hp shunter. Introduced into traffic from the mid 1950s to replace steam at various goods yards, carriage sidings and principal stations, several are still in traffic on the same duties today, some fifty-plus years later, which certainly says something about their reliability. All of the major locomotive and goods depots had at least a couple of 08s allocated throughout the 1960s and 1970s for use as yard pilots. Light goods turns were also commonplace earlier in their career. Typical spots they could expect to be seen were Eastfield Traction Maintenance Depot, Cadder and Mossend marshalling yards, and the quayside lines around the Prince's Dock and General Terminus iron ore terminal on the south banks of the Clyde.

During the mid 1980s, Eastfield depot's resident 08s were bulled up with various livery variations, like many of the main line diesels allocated there. They were the yard pilots after all and were treated as such! Over the next few years, 08938 became a celebrity machine, painted in an alternative Railfreight grey livery with white roof and yellow cabsides, plus the 'Scottie Dog' depot mascot and 'ED' (the TOPS depot code) painted prominently on its bodysides. BR blue with black roofs and small 'Scottie Dogs' were carried by all 08430/720/853. For a long time, 08s have also been used as pilots at Deanside Transit goods depot near Cardonald, carrying various colourful liveries over the years for the haulage company J.G. Russell.

Today's operations include a pair of 08s – 08568/730 – based for shunting duties at Springburn works operated by Knorr-Bremse Rail Systems (formerly Railcare), though the former has been stored out of service for some time. For a few years, both carried a special two-tone grey livery and the unofficial names *St Rollox* and *The Caley* respectively. A striking green, grey and blue Knorr-Bremse colour scheme is now carried by 08730. There is also still usually an 08 pilot based at both Polmadie depot and Mossend Yard at the time of writing.

Main line diesels: Type 1 (1,000bhp or below)

The unsuccessful Clayton Class 17s spent much of their very short working lives around the Glasgow area, with Polmadie depot having a significant allocation. They were employed on a wide variety of mixed goods work, though generally working double-headed due to their relatively low horsepower and tendency to fail. Occasional passenger work was generally restricted to extras where nothing else was available, such as football or race specials, using mostly suburban compartment rolling stock. Ultimately, the Claytons' troublesome engines and unusual single centre-cab layout did not endear them to crews and saw them withdrawn in favour of the more successful Class 20s. The last were taken out of traffic only a few years after they were built, and subsequently lengthy rows of condemned locomotives became a common sight at various depots on the region.

English Electric Class 20s were a frequent sight all over Glasgow from the 1960s right up until the early 1990s. In the beginning, locomotives were mostly allocated to Eastfield, Polmadie and Motherwell depots, being used on all manner of mixed and block freight workings. Except in their earlier years, the class nearly always ran

The rare visit of a loco-hauled train to Exhibition Centre station, on 30 September 2013, with DRS Class 20s Nos 20308/309 stopping off on Pathfinder Railtours' 'Autumn Highlander' tour from Pitlochry and Fort William. Opened in 1979 as Finnieston, the unusual V-shaped platforms here replaced the original 1894-built Stobcross station. (Author's collection)

double-headed, with typical duties including oil traffic to Grangemouth and coal and iron ore to Ravenscraig steelworks. Speedlink wagonload traffic out of Mossend was gradually handed over to Class 37 haulage as the 20 fleet was run down. Eastfield and Motherwell were the last depots to have an allocation of the locomotives.

Class 20s largely disappeared from Scotland in the early 1990s, bar the small Hunslet–Barclay 20/9 fleet used on occasional weedkiller trains. However, privatisation saw Direct Rail Services (DRS) start to bring the occasional refurbished 20/3 north of the border. The early 2000s saw nuclear-flask trains between Carlisle Kingmoor and Hunterston, on the Ayrshire coast, regularly produce a pair of them, routed via the WCML and Shields Junction–Paisley. The DRS fleet has since shrunk to just a handful of locomotives, though at the time of writing the same duty can occasionally produce a pair of 20s, or a 20 double-headed with a 37.

Type 2 (1,001–1,499bhp)

Both variants of Sulzer Type 2s, Class 24 and 25, were regularly seen in the Glasgow area throughout the 1960s and 1970s. The 24s generally played second fiddle to their later-built cousins, being used on some of the lighter freight duties out of Cadder Yard to destinations such as Grangemouth and Falkland Yard, Ayr. Inverness–Glasgow passenger trains and some short-distance parcels traffic also kept the 24s busy, before most were withdrawn from traffic rather prematurely in the late 1970s.

The 25s lasted longer, with a mass exodus of locomotives to Eastfield and Haymarket depots during the mid 1970s to replace the 24s. Eastfield had its first allocation of 25s in 1966, made up of D7611–23, which were used mainly on freight due to not having steam-heat boilers. The depot received a number of boiler-fitted 25s over the next decade, mainly to work passenger trains from Glasgow Queen Street–Oban/Fort William/Perth/Dundee, as well as various specials. For some time, 25s would also provide the power on some petroleum traffic originating at Grangemouth, serving the depots at Bishopbriggs and Bowling, and double-heading on the heavy workings to Dalmarnock and Braehead power stations.

Replacement of Type 2s with Class 37s and 47s into the 1980s saw 25s largely disappear from Scotland, though three (25305/10/4) were converted to ETHEL Electric Train Heating units in 1983 for use on the West Highland Line. Given the departmental numbers 97250–52, they were coupled next to Class 37s on the morning Down and evening Up trains between Glasgow Queen Street and Fort William to provide heat for the through sleeping cars from London Euston. Introduction of Electric Train Heat (ETH)-fitted Class 37/4s in 1985 saw them transferred south of the border for other duties.

Since the 25s were nicknamed 'Rats', the almost entirely Scottish-based BRCW Class 26s became 'MacRats'! After Queen Street became the terminus serving Inverness in 1966, services to the Highland capital normally employed the locomotives double-headed, while they were also regularly used on shorter-distance passenger workings to Perth or Dundee. Type 2s were less common at Glasgow Central, though the early 1980s saw 26s appear regularly on some Glasgow–Carlisle via Dumfries passenger workings.

The withdrawal of Class 25s and 27s during the mid 1980s saw many 26s re-allocated to Eastfield TMD and used more on freight traffic, while 47s and DMUs took over their passenger turns. Speedlink duties out of Mossend saw the class operate to destinations as widespread as Inverness, Grangemouth and Lugton. In the early 1990s, the 26 fleet was also run down and the class was relegated mostly to engineers trains. Closure of Eastfield in 1992 would see the remaining locomotives move to Inverness before the last examples were withdrawn in October 1993.

Their higher-powered relatives, the Class 27s, were a regular sight in the north of Glasgow in particular, either on passenger workings from Queen Street or goods turns from Cadder Yard. They had sole command of the Glasgow–Fort William/Mallaig/Oban routes after the withdrawal of Class 29s in 1971, by which time most class members were now based at Eastfield. Their new employment on the Glasgow–Edinburgh express services that same year saw the creation of the 27/1 sub-class; denoting locomotives dual-braked and fitted with push–pull equipment. Twenty-four examples were eventually converted, before twelve had Electric Train Heating alternators added to become 27/2s. The use of one locomotive at each end of a six-coach train meant fast turnarounds at Queen Street and Edinburgh Waverley in keeping with the high-speed timetable.

Class 27s were also regulars on freight traffic south of the Clyde from the mid 1960s onwards. New passenger diagrams for them in the early 1980s were Glasgow Central–Stranraer/Carlisle services, before Class 47s took these over a few years later. They had surrendered their Glasgow–Edinburgh and West Highland duties early in the decade, becoming very much freight-only machines by this point. Mass withdrawals beckoned and by August 1987 all of the class had been withdrawn from service.

The NBL Type 2s, constructed in Springburn, failed to match the high standards set by the Derby- and Birmingham-built Bo-Bos (classes 24, 25, 26, 27). The TOPS operating system classified them as Class 21, though twenty of the fifty-eight machines had their MAN power units replaced by Paxman types to become Class 29. The original examples had a high failure rate and tended to work in multiple on passenger trains along Glasgow–Aberdeen/Dundee/Fort William/Oban, before most were stored and subsequently scrapped at McWilliam's Metals in Garrowhill after very short careers. The re-engined

Class 29s were more reliable but still much below par. They worked most trains single-handed, with passenger workings generally restricted to the West Highland lines or Glasgow–Perth. Freight workings saw them potter around Cadder Yard and the central belt for a few years before the last examples were withdrawn in 1971.

Type 3 (1,500–1,999bhp)

Early allocations of English Electric Class 37s in Scotland from 1966 included locomotives allocated to Polmadie, Motherwell and Eastfield depots. They were usually dedicated to heavy bulk trains, often working in pairs taking coal towards Fife and the central belt, oil to Bowling, Bishopbriggs and Hawkhead, as well as steel from Ravenscraig, near Motherwell. It was not until 1981 that they started to gain regular passenger work north of the border, when many examples fitted with steam-heat boilers were cascaded north to Eastfield to replace Class 27s on the lines to Oban, Fort William and Mallaig.

In 1985, thirty-one of the steam-heat 37/0s were refurbished to carry Electric Train Heating generators for work on the West Highland lines, with Nos 37401–13

One of Eastfield's split-headcode Class 37/0s passes the burnt-out shell of Maryhill Park signal box with a train from the West Highlands in July 1982. The box caught fire and was closed in 1980, never being replaced. The new Maryhill station is now situated behind the cameraman. (Allan Trotter, Eastbank Model Railway Club)

and 37422–25 based at Eastfield and repainted in the popular BR 'Large Logo' colour scheme. Other 37/4s would later be cascaded to Scotland to join them, but the majority of the original seventeen continued to work in that area for most of their careers. The 1980s had also seen the 37s expand on to other routes, working more Railfreight Speedlink traffic from Mossend to the yards at Inverness, Aberdeen and Ayr amongst others.

A famous traffic flow diagrammed for pairs of Type 3s was iron ore and coal between Hunterston and Ravenscraig steelworks, near Motherwell, until the latter closed in 1992. A number of 37/3s (re-bogied sub-class, with train heat boilers removed and fuel capacity extended) were based at Motherwell TMD along with some 37/0s to haul these trains, which were often *triple*-headed for part of their journey. A third 37 was usually added to each loaded train at Mossend to tackle the formidable 1 in 86 gradient towards Ravenscraig terminal, making these workings a particular favourite with photographers.

After losing most of their West Highland passenger work to Sprinters in January 1989, Eastfield's 37/4s joined the other sub-classes on more freight work, though they continued to haul the Fort William portion of the London Euston sleeper for a long time after this. ScotRail 'Young Explorer' trains gave them new passenger work, in the summer only, from 1992 to 1994, working from Glasgow Queen Street to Oban and Fort William. On the freight side, two refurbished Railfreight Petroleum sub-sector 37/7s – 37707/708 – were transferred to Eastfield for a short period in November 1989 to work a daily Bulklink freight service between Millerhill Yard, Edinburgh, and Inverness. However, freight work for 37s in Scotland was soon on the decline following the abolition of the Speedlink network and the closure of Ravenscraig. The closure of Eastfield depot saw its 37s re-allocated to either Inverness or Motherwell.

Privatisation saw increased numbers of Class 56s and 60s taking over Class 37 turns, particularly coal traffic, but it was the 1998 introduction of Class 66s that was the death knell for most of the type on freight work, by now owned by the English Welsh and Scottish Railway (EWS). By 2001, 37/0s, 37/5s and 37/7s were becoming few and far between, and the only class members still based in Scotland were the 37/4s used for the Fort William sleeper and the odd Enterprise freight working, though DRS locomotives regularly visited from south of the border, mainly pairs of locomotives still diagrammed for the daily Daventry–Grangemouth intermodal.

The Motherwell RETB (Radio Electronic Token Block)-fitted 37/4 fleet gradually dwindled in size, especially after June 2006 when Class 67s took over the Fort William sleeper. Still, the fleet plodded on for a few more years, proving useful for charters and engineering trains on lines with low route availability where Class 66s were not permitted, such as to Oban or Milngavie. June 2010 saw the last EWS (now DB Schenker) Class 37 workings to Scotland when

37425 worked MoD and ballast trains from Mossend to the West Highland Line. DRS and West Coast Railways Class 37s have visited Glasgow regularly since. At the time of writing, DRS machines still often work the weekly nuclear-flask train to Hunterston and occasionally deputise for Class 66s on other diagrams. Happily, this includes some of the fondly remembered West Highland locomotives that were once the pride and joy of Eastfield depot.

Type 4 (2,000–2,999bhp)

Class 40s took over the majority of WCML expresses in and out of Glasgow Central from steam locomotives and proved themselves to be a good match for the big LMS 'Duchess' Pacifics. The 40s' reign there proved to be short-lived, as Class 47s and 50s took over most of these duties in the late 1960s. However, Haymarket depot's batch of locomotives (D260–66 and D357–68) became regulars on Glasgow Queen Street–Aberdeen three-hour expresses after the closure of Buchanan Street station and withdrawal of the last LNER A4 Pacifics. They proved themselves to be far more capable performers than the NBL Type 2s, which were originally planned to replace steam on this route and went on to dominate these workings until the coming of more 47s to Scotland in the late 1970s.

Class 40s also appeared on a variety of freight traffic after losing their WCML passenger turns. Booked workings through the 1970s included the 6S41 Haverton Hill–Grangemouth, 6S52 Windsford–Cadder Yard and 6M82 Gunnie–Pennyfordd cement train. Freight traffic continued until most of the Scottish-based locomotives were moved south of the border at the start of the 1980s.

High Speed Trains (HST), otherwise known as InterCity 125s (with Class 43 power cars at each end), first appeared in the Glasgow area in the 1980s, when for a few years there were daily through-services between Glasgow Queen Street and London King's Cross. Other InterCity expresses that took them to Queen Street in the 1980s included 'The Cornishman', which was a daily Glasgow–Penzance return Monday–Friday, extending to and from Newquay on summer Saturdays.

The 1990s saw HSTs become a regular sight at Glasgow Central when they took over various InterCity cross-country workings operating to destinations such as Bournemouth and Penzance. After privatisation, Virgin took over these services, with most sets being made up of seven coaches. In addition, the Virgin CrossCountry fleet included several power cars that were buffer-fitted, having been formerly used as driving van trailers (DVTs) on the East Coast Main Line.

Despite the new Virgin Voyager 'Operation Princess' timetable switchover in September 2002, some HSTs remained in service and still operated into Central until September the following year. Since then, the Network Rail New Measurement Train – formed of a refurbished HST set using power cars

43013/4/62 – has been a regular visitor to lines all over Glasgow, including many that are virtually DMU or EMU-only. In addition, the new CrossCountry franchise operates a small fleet of HSTs (currently ten power cars) that can appear on services rostered for Voyager units.

The Class 45 and 46 'Peak' diesels were a familiar sight on expresses from Glasgow St Enoch to Leeds, Sheffield, Nottingham and London St Pancras, such as the Thames–Clyde Express, which used the GSWR main line via Dumfries and the former Midland Railway Anglo-Scottish route south of the border. The closure of St Enoch station would subsequently see these trains transferred to Glasgow Central. 'Peaks' were still a regular sight on these workings well into the 1970s, together with some slower Glasgow–Carlisle via Dumfries services, though the Thames–Clyde ceased to operate in 1976. Following a period of decline and replacement by Class 47s and HSTs, the next time 'Peaks' would be seen in Glasgow would be when many of them were cut up at MC Metals in Springburn during the late 1980s and early 1990s.

As with the 37s, Class 47s are another type to have a long-standing association with Glasgow, and one which still continues to this day. Originally classified as

On 18 August 1987, 47/7 No. 47703 *Saint Mungo* powers away from Glasgow Queen Street towards Cowlairs Tunnel, with the 0925 to Aberdeen. The leading coach is a non-air-conditioned Mark 2, which is unusual for a push–pull working. (Jules Hathaway)

Brush Type 4s, the first 47s to see regular use in the city were based at Polmadie shed, working West Coast Main Line passenger services along with Class 50s prior to electrification, as well as some Anglo-Scottish goods, such as new Freightliner container flows from Gushetfaulds in the south side. The mid 1970s saw them start to be used on more inter-regional passenger work when a number of locomotives were sent to Eastfield depot, and in 1979 they started to take over many Type 2 diagrams, such as Glasgow–Edinburgh and Glasgow–Inverness/Aberdeen. This resulted in the 47/7 sub-class fitted with push–pull equipment for use on the Edinburgh and Aberdeen trains. The first twelve of these were converted in 1979 for the Edinburgh route, with 47713–16 subsequently added to the fleet in 1985 when push–pull commenced to Aberdeen. All initially carried BR blue or 'Large Logo' livery before receiving ScotRail colours to match the coaching stock.

In the mid 1980s, 47s also began work on Glasgow Central–Stranraer/Carlisle via Dumfries services. By now, the big Sulzer-engined machines were by far the

Push–pull fitted Class 47/7s

47701	Saint Andrew
47702	Saint Cuthbert
47703	Saint Mungo
47704	Dunedin
47705	Lothian
47706	Strathclyde
47707	Holyrood
47708	Waverley
47709	The Lord Provost
47710	Sir Walter Scott
47711	Greyfriars Bobby
47712	Lady Diana Spencer
47713	Tayside Region
47714	Grampian Region
47715	Haymarket
47716	Duke of Edinburgh's Award
47717	Tayside Region*

* 47717 was a new locomotive added to the fleet in 1988 after 47713 was withdrawn due to fire damage, gaining its nameplates in the process.

dominant type of traction seen hauling passenger trains north of the border and for the most part these were the ETH-fitted 47/4 variants. Speedlink freights also took the class to all corners of the country, working out of Mossend. However, 47s gave way to Sprinters on the Stranraer and Carlisle services in October 1988, while 1990 saw them also lose their passenger work to Edinburgh, Aberdeen and Inverness. From this point onwards, they became largely freight-only machines throughout Scotland.

The 1990s would see mass withdrawals of 47s, though some were retained at Motherwell depot for freight duties, as well as a handful of locomotives dedicated to sleeper services to Inverness and Aberdeen from 1998. EWS gained the Rail Express Systems (RES) fleet of a new 47/7 sub-class, which worked out of Glasgow Central on postal duties, while Freightliner locomotives could be seen working car traffic out of Mossend and Coatbridge. EWS 47/7s and Virgin 47/8s provided the motive power for WCML services out of Glasgow Central on the rare occasions of overhead line problems or diversions via the GSWR main line. Most of the aforementioned duties had come to an end by 2004, and Class 47s have been a rare sight around Glasgow ever since, with most appearances now restricted to special charters, using DRS or West Coast Railways locomotives.

All fifty of the English Electric Class 50s (originally numbered D400–449) were commonly seen working over the West Coast Main Line into Glasgow Central prior to that line's electrification. They started regularly operating

An almost brand-new Class 50 No. D410 runs light past Polmadie, heading towards the engine shed in June 1968. TOPS renumbering saw the locomotive become 50010 *Monarch*. (Allan Trotter, Eastbank Model Railway Club)

double-headed from 1970 after upgrades to the permanent way allowed higher running speeds, with all of the class now fitted with multiple-working jumper cables. Diversions from the main route also took them via the Cathcart Circle and GSWR main line; the latter accessed via Paisley Gilmour Street and Dalry. WCML services to Perth and Inverness also regularly took the class over the Motherwell–Cumbernauld route, while those operating into Glasgow Central were maintained at Polmadie depot, though allocated to Crewe.

Nicknamed 'Hoovers' by enthusiasts, the 50s were made redundant by West Coast electrification in 1974 and soon disappeared altogether from Scotland, though they were to gain a new lease of life, being transferred to the Western Region of BR, and were all named after famous warships. After this, occasional railtours would still bring the class back to Glasgow, even after their withdrawal by BR, with preserved machines 50031 *Hood*, 50033 *Glorious*, 50049 *Defiance* and 50050 *Fearless* having all visited at the time of writing.

Type 5 (3,000bhp+)

While the LMS 'Duchess' Pacifics had LNER A4s as their rivals over on the East Coast Main Line, the Class 50's equivalent nemesis in the early diesel era was undoubtedly the Class 55 'Deltic'. The odd Glasgow Queen St–King's Cross through-service could produce a 'Deltic' on occasions, as could the occasional special. BR 'Merrymaker' Sunday excursions from Edinburgh to Oban unusually produced a 'Deltic' on both 2 and 23 August 1981 during the class' dying days in traffic. In addition to that, the preservation era would see numerous appearances by the main line-certified trio 55009 *Alycidon,* 55019 *Royal Highland Fusilier* and 55022 *Royal Scots Grey* on railtours.

'Deltic' No. 55022 *Royal Scots Grey* lays a smokescreen across Bellgrove station on the North Clyde line, heading towards Springburn works with two translator coaches for another EMU move, 11 January 2014. (Author's collection)

Still, few could have predicted the events of 2013, which saw 55022 hired by GB Railfreight (GBRf) for a contract hauling ScotRail EMUs on empty coaching stock moves around the city! What's more, Springburn works actually became the locomotive's home depot for a lengthy period following its arrival there on 24 April. The BR blue-liveried 'Deltic' – hired in due to a longstanding locomotive shortage with GBRf – was used several times a week, hauling Class 318 and 334 units between their home depots at Yoker and Shields Road, and the works at Springburn and Bonnyton, Kilmarnock, where they were undergoing refurbishment. This saw 55022 become a regular if unusual sight all over the electrified city suburban network. These duties still continue at the time of writing and may do for some time yet, as the English Electric machine's performance so far with GBRf has been nothing short of outstanding.

Around 1993, Railfreight Class 56s started to become established on both Anglo-Scottish and domestic coal traffic, working from Ravenstruther loading terminal in Lanarkshire and various destinations in Ayrshire. Privatisation in 1994 saw thirteen locomotives operated by TransRail reallocated to Motherwell TMD for a variety of traffic, including Hunterston–Longannet power station coal and Mossend–Grangemouth oil traffic. The Motherwell–Cumbernauld route was the prime place to view the class on such workings, while they also headed south over the WCML on Enterprises. This included regular visits to Deanside Transit, near Cardonald, with the heavy Wisbech–Deanside van trains.

Unfortunately, the EWS era saw 56s gradually phased out north of the border, with their last booked duties in 2002 being Enterprise workings from Mossend to Perth, Aberdeen and Doncaster. After an early retirement for the entire class in 2004, it would not be until the summer of 2013, nearly a decade later, that another would return to Scotland on a freight train. This was on the Linkswood–Grangemouth–Prestwick aviation fuel circuit, which has since featured regular haulage by Colas Rail's small 56 fleet after a period of Class 66 monopoly.

Class 47s re-engined and renumbered as Class 57s have been seen around Glasgow in various forms since 2002, when Virgin's initial fleet of twelve (later extended to sixteen) 57/3 locomotives started to replace Class 47s on diversions and as standby locomotives along the WCML. The latter duty soon saw one locomotive at a time out-based at Polmadie, with all of the fleet given names of *Thunderbirds* television characters. After most of the West Coast Route Modernisation work finished, GBRf then started regularly hiring a 57/3 to haul empty ScotRail EMUs to and from Springburn works on the same duties which later employed 'Deltic' 55022. The company also used them occasionally to haul dead Class 325 EMUs on postal trains from Shieldmuir.

DRS has its own fleet of 57s, either ex-Freightliner 57/0s or Virgin 57/3s. They sometimes operate in pairs on the Carlisle–Hunterston nuclear-flasks, or on intermodal traffic from Coatbridge or Grangemouth in place of Class 66s.

West Coast Railways' fleet of 57s also pass through the city on charter trains and the Royal Scotsman luxury landcruise.

After introduction to traffic in 1990, the hugely powerful Class 60s were trialled instead of double-headed 37s on the Hunterston–Ravenscraig iron ore trains. Late in the 1990s, they became a regular sight around Mossend and Motherwell depot, with the daily Dalzell–Lackenby steel train a regular diagram. Oil traffic took them from Mossend to Grangemouth, Prestwick and Dalston on a daily basis, as well as a variety of coal, Enterprise and engineers workings. However, the years that followed saw use of 60s north of the border decline sharply, with Class 66s gradually taking over most of these turns. Changing market factors were also to blame, with the recent recession and the resultant loss of rail freight traffic seeing most of the hundred-strong Class 60 fleet placed into store by DB Schenker. Happily, a recent change in attitude by the company has seen many of them overhauled and reinstated, but the class have long been absent from Scotland.

General Motors Class 66s are now by far and away the staple freight machines to be seen in the Glasgow area, or anywhere in the UK. The EWS 66/0 fleet started to be commonly seen from introduction in 1998, firstly taking over merry-go-round coal workings (such as the frequent Hunterston–Longannet circuit) from 37s, 56s and 60s. Freightliner Heavy Haul's 66/5s and 66/6s appeared soon after on competing Anglo-Scottish coal workings and other traffic such as Crewe–Mossend car-carrying trains and cement from Viewpark (Uddingston)–Oxwellmains. GBRf's 66/7 fleet was also sometimes hired by Freightliner. Furthermore, the DRS 66/4 fleet became a regular sight on container traffic from 2003, starting with the Grangemouth–Daventry and Coatbridge–Daventry flows.

Today, the only freight serving customers in Glasgow that has not gone over to Class 66 haulage is certain Anglo-Scottish traffic that utilises fast electric traction over the WCML. Virtually all internal traffic throughout Scotland uses the big Type 5 diesels, even though all machines are now maintained at depots south of the border. As well as the commonly seen DRS, Freightliner and DB Schenker (EWS) locomotives, GBRf's 66/7s can now also be seen on a daily basis hauling Fort William–North Blyth bulk alumina workings, running via Stepps and Coatbridge, while Colas Rail 66/8s have hauled Grangemouth–Prestwick oil traffic via Cumbernauld and Paisley.

EWS's fleet of thirty Class 67 Bo-Bos were originally dedicated solely to postal and express parcels traffic centred around Mossend and Shieldmuir Royal Mail terminal. They worked trains daily to Aberdeen and Inverness to the north, and Walsall and London to the south. Royal Mail's decision to cease using rail traffic saw EWS's 67 fleet suddenly become spare for other duties, resulting in more freight and passenger work for the class. More charter trains started to use 67 haulage after the mass withdrawal of many 37s and 47s, while their June 2006 introduction on the West Highland Line saw them used not only on the Caledonian Sleeper but also MoD traffic between Mossend and Glen Douglas. Other freights regularly using 67s were workings from Mossend to Inverness, Irvine and Deanside Transit. Today, the 67s are virtually passenger-only and, as well as regular charters and the Fort William sleeper, they are found frequently working the empty stock of the Glasgow–London Euston 'Lowland' sleeper between Central station and Polmadie depot.

First-generation diesel multiple units

The Metro-Cammell Class 101s are probably the 'heritage' DMU class most associated with the Glasgow area. The earliest examples used were on the Glasgow Buchanan Street–Dundee circuit in the late 1950s, before they established themselves further on other routes over the next two decades to replace other, less successful DMU types. Their heyday was undoubtedly the 1980s, when the class could be seen departing every few minutes on local workings in and out of both Queen Street and Central stations, all working in three-car formations. From Queen Street they operated to Dunblane, Stirling and Perth, as well as between Springburn and Cumbernauld. From Central, they served Barrhead, Kilmarnock, East Kilbride, Kilmacolm and Edinburgh via Shotts, as well as Largs and Ayr prior to electrification of those lines.

Widespread Sprinter introduction saw the Met-Camm DMUs displaced from said duties in the early 1990s, though a small number of them were redeployed on Glasgow–Paisley Canal services instead of 156s. They were also later rostered for Glasgow–Barrhead and new Glasgow–Whifflet workings from 1993, with a small fleet of units based at Corkerhill, comprising of 101684/6–95. All were now reduced to two-car, power-twin units and painted in Strathclyde PTE livery. In 1996, 101692 was repainted in a special 'Caledonian Blue' colour scheme, as the 101s were put to use on another new SPT route: Motherwell to Cumbernauld. The 'heritage' DMUs would not last forever though, and July 2000 saw the last 101s withdrawn from Corkerhill, having managed to outlast all other first-generation units in the area by quite some margin. Their departure also marked the last use of slam-door rolling stock on Glasgow suburban services.

A number of BRCW Class 104 three-car units saw use out of both Central and Queen Street stations during the 1980s, when several were transferred north to either Ayr or Eastfield depots, principally to replace Class 107s written off following a fire at Ayr. They were used on all of the same local workings that used Class 101s and 107s, though a large number were hybrid units, which used one or more vehicles of other DMU classes. There were, for example, several 104s running with 101 centre cars, or even units with a 104 driving vehicle at one end and a 101 or 105 at the other. Those which were complete 104 sets were mostly still painted in all-over BR blue when they were withdrawn from service in 1989, though a few were blue and grey. An interesting exception was two-car 104325, which was painted in a unique maroon and white livery for working on the Crianlarich–Oban line and nicknamed 'The Mexican Bean'. It was very much confined to that route but was maintained at Eastfield depot.

Cravens Class 105 two-cars initially worked Glasgow Central–Hamilton Circle–Lanark services prior to electrification in 1974, but reached other destinations after then, mainly as hybrid units. Some three-car sets were formed with a single 105 trailer car and two 101 vehicles, seeing work from Glasgow Central–Edinburgh via Shotts, Kilmacolm and Ayr. In 1983 the remaining few units were withdrawn, though a few vehicles saw use again for a short period in 1986 to cover for stock shortages after the Ayr depot fire.

The twenty-six 'Derby Heavyweight' Class 107 DMUs spent most of their careers working local services around Glasgow and sharing certain routes with other classes such as 101s and 120s. All three-car units, they worked Glasgow–Largs/Ayr services along with other types such as 101s once Class 126s had been

On 27 November 1987, Class 107 No. 107439 leaves Barrhead on a Glasgow Central–Kilmarnock service. The unit, based at Ayr depot, still carries 'Trans-Clyde' branding. (David Webster)

withdrawn, often combining to form six- or even nine-car trains. Class 107s were also frequent performers on the lines to Kilmacolm, Barrhead, Kilmarnock and Edinburgh via Shotts. Fifteen examples subsequently received Strathclyde PTE orange and black livery in the mid 1980s. The class were regulars at Queen Street station too, being utilised on services to Falkirk Grahamston, Dunblane, Stirling and Perth. Whilst the coming of the Class 156s and 158s saw the 107s' workload reduced, they were not fully displaced from duties out of Queen Street until July 1991, when the last of the Eastfield-allocated sets were sent to Edinburgh Haymarket.

The mid–late 1980s was undoubtedly the most interesting period for DMU fans in Glasgow, despite most classes being in the twilight of their careers. The adoption of Strathclyde PTE's own house colours and a mini-revival of the old BR 'corporate blue' meant that there was more livery variation than there had been for a long time. Furthermore, rather than each suburban route being totally dominated by one particular class, any DMU diagram was very much a free-for-all. One day a service train could be worked by a 101, the next day a 107 and the day after a Class 120, so it was all very unpredictable and exciting for the enthusiast.

Among the other classes that were acquired second-hand from English depots were the 'Derby Lightweight' Class 108s and Swindon Cross-Country Class 120s. Both could be seen regularly working out of Queen Street and Central during the second half of the 1980s, with the latter typically working to Edinburgh via Shotts. Class 116s were a resident Scottish type, with Hamilton depot once having fourteen of them during the 1970s for workings to Lanark and the Hamilton Circle. Latterly they moved between Ayr, Corkerhill and Eastfield depots and covered a variety of local services, before the last were withdrawn or transferred away during 1987.

The Swindon Cross-Country InterCity Class 126s were built specially for use on both the Edinburgh and Glasgow main line and the Ayrshire coast. These three-car units had a distinctive look, with a different style of cab at each end. One cab end had a corridor connection through the middle, with the idea that two units would normally be joined to run in six-car formations. The fleet used on Glasgow Queen Street–Edinburgh Waverley services was made up of sixty-four cars, including eight buffet vehicles, and entered traffic in 1957. Ayr depot received a later batch of units in 1959 to work services from Glasgow to Ayr, Largs, Ardrossan, Girvan and Stranraer; with sixty-eight cars in all, including two buffets.

It was ironic that these unreliable units, which were purpose-built for their designated routes, were replaced relatively soon after by locomotive-hauled trains drafted in from elsewhere. After their 1971 replacement on the E&G line by Class 27s, the rest of the Scottish 126s survived, working in Ayrshire, until the last were withdrawn in 1983. The previous year had seen Glasgow–Stranraer services return to loco-haulage. Fortunately, one of the class (car Nos 51017/51043/59404 plus buffet vehicle 79443) survives in preservation at the Bo'ness and Kinneil Railway as a reminder of how BR InterCity travel once was.

Second-generation diesel multiple units

Class 156 Sprinter units have been a familiar sight operating out of Central and Queen Street stations since 1988. October that year saw them replace Class 47s on Glasgow–Stranraer/Carlisle workings and first-generation units on Glasgow–Barrhead/Kilmarnock/East Kilbride, being based at Corkerhill depot. In 1989, Haymarket-based sets took over Glasgow–Oban/Fort William/Mallaig workings and fourteen units (156501–14) painted in Strathclyde PTE orange and black were added to the Corkerhill allocation. The years to come would see the routes to Cumbernauld, Whifflet, Paisley Canal, Edinburgh via Shotts and Anniesland via Maryhill also go over to 156s.

The Scottish-based 156 fleet covers much the same duties today. The recent electrification of the Paisley Canal, Whifflet and Cumbernauld lines will free up more 156s for duties between Glasgow–Oban, which will have its service frequency doubled from summer 2014. Combined Glasgow–Oban/Mallaig services often run as six-car formations, while four-car formations are common on most city suburban routes. The more lightly-loaded trains such as Glasgow–Anniesland are usually single two-car units.

The Strathclyde PTE orange livery eventually gave way to the attractive carmine and cream SPT-branded colours; 156443, named *The Kilmarnock Edition*, carried a unique version of this livery for many years, with a light grey roof and cream colour extended on to the cab ends. Another unique unit was Central Trains-liveried 156403, which ScotRail borrowed for the summer 2007 timetable. Blue ScotRail Saltire livery is the dominant colour scheme today.

In 1990, Class 158 units took over most passenger duties out of Glasgow Queen Street, operating mainly to Edinburgh, Aberdeen and Inverness, either as two- or four-car formations, though it took some time for ScotRail to gain full availability of the fleet (based at Haymarket depot) following a few teething troubles during their first year in traffic. Most notably, January 1991 saw every one of the units temporarily withdrawn from traffic for a couple of days to solve problems arising from loose water pumps.

After this, the 158s enjoyed a fruitful decade on the region and proved to have an excellent reliability record. After the new millennium, nearly all Glasgow–Edinburgh diagrams went over to Class 170s. Trains to Inverness and Aberdeen would also see large-scale 170 deployment, though 158s still continue on some workings to this day. As a result of these changes, 158s have been re-diagrammed on many short-distance routes, with ScotRail units now based at either Haymarket or Inverness. Glasgow Queen Street–Anniesland/Falkirk Grahamston/Stirling/Perth/Alloa are now regular duties for the class, and recent years have seen them begin regular use again out of Glasgow Central as well, on services to Whifflet and Edinburgh via Shotts.

Prior to that, between 1999 and 2003, two-car units operated by Northern Spirit (latterly Arriva Trains Northern) could be seen at Central on a daily return service from Leeds–Glasgow. In addition, recent years have seen 158s from other operators loaned to ScotRail. This has made for the unusual sight of South West Trains livery at Anniesland and Wessex at Cumbernauld!

Class 158s are also known to be paired with Class 170s from time to time on services out of Queen Street. The initial batch of twenty-six 170s, christened 'Turbostars', were put to work on Glasgow–Edinburgh/Inverness/Aberdeen services and proved so successful that ScotRail ordered many more for other routes. Seven units were subsequently painted in SPT carmine and cream livery for local services from Glasgow Queen Street–Falkirk Grahamston/Dunblane/Falkirk/Stirling, though they have now been painted into ScotRail Saltire blue like the rest of the class. Most Turbostars now carry first-class accommodation in one coach, with another recent innovation being wi-fi for passengers. All are

A contrast of past and present ScotRail colour schemes at Bishopbriggs on 6 January 2014, as two local services pass. Saltire-liveried 170393 drops off passengers on the 1148 Glasgow Queen Street–Stirling, while First-liveried 170411 waits with the 1123 Stirling–Glasgow. (Author's collection)

three-car units, though they are regularly combined as six cars on peak-time services from Glasgow to Edinburgh.

While the introduction of short-length Virgin Voyager units on the WCML looked like a measure to economise, the start of Siemens Desiro Class 185 operation in 2007 took this to the next level. TransPennine Express started using these three-car units (fifty-one built in total) on Glasgow–Manchester Airport services in December 2007, taking over a route previously operated by Virgin CrossCountry. The 185s have an external appearance more akin to that of a suburban unit, so they look rather out of place today operating on the WCML south of Glasgow. However, their swift acceleration, coming from three engines per set (one in each car), results in fast journey times, the quickest being around three-and-a-half hours each way.

Diesel-electric multiple units

Class 220 Voyagers started to be seen on regular Virgin CrossCountry diagrams out of Glasgow Central in the early part of 2002. By the start of the much-publicised 'Operation Princess' timetable that September, they had taken over nearly all former Class 86 and HST workings; the main routes of which were Glasgow–Birmingham/Bristol/Bournemouth/Plymouth/Poole/Penzance. Controversially, many Voyagers worked these as just single four-car units despite the long distances, hence the complaints about overcrowding. Later, eight-car formations became more common. Whilst not exactly popular with rail enthusiasts, the Voyagers did at least benefit from an imaginative naming policy, Scottish-themed examples including *Clyde Voyager* (220006), *Lanarkshire Voyager* (220012) and *Solway Voyager* (220015).

The similar Class 221 Super Voyagers entered Virgin CrossCountry service around the same time and offered a tilting mechanism at higher speeds similar to the electric Pendolinos. In addition, forty out of the forty-four units built were five-car sets; the rest four-car. Following the start of the new CrossCountry franchise (operated by Arriva) in December 2007, most 220s and 221s were passed over to the new company, who eventually painted the units in their own maroon and silver colour scheme. Today, Arriva CrossCountry operates all of the Voyagers and twenty-three Super Voyagers, while Virgin retain twenty Super Voyagers for Edinburgh/Glasgow–Birmingham services. The WCML remains the main stamping ground for both types, though they have also been seen on the Hamilton and Cathcart Circles, the Holytown and Wishaw loop, Motherwell–Cumbernauld and the GSWR main line, either on diversions or route-learning turns.

7

Electric Traction

The drive for faster services has seen electric traction take over the lion's share of work on Glasgow's railways, and in the next few years there will be more to come. Yet the electrics are not a novelty; the gradual electrification of the city network started back in the late 1950s with the 'Blue Trains'. The following classes of locomotive and multiple unit have been dominant in the period of electric traction.

There were five different classes among the first BR electric locomotives ordered for use on the WCML, which all had the prefix 'AL' (AL1/AL2/AL3/AL4/AL5).

At Glasgow Central, Class 85 No. 85006 is pictured at the head of the 1245 service to Cardiff. At Carstairs, another portion of the train will join from Edinburgh Waverley. 7 May 1986. (Jules Hathaway)

These later became Class 81, 82, 83, 84 and 85. There was only a small batch built of each, with BR experimenting with different designs following the 1955 Modernisation Plan, as they were with the diesels. Each class was built by a different manufacturer, with the ten Class 84s built in Glasgow by the North British Locomotive Co. in Springburn, which up until that point had had little experience of producing electrics.

After the extension of West Coast electrification to Glasgow, Class 87s controlled most of the London Euston expresses, while the earlier-built classes 81–85 tended to be used on other Anglo-Scottish workings such as Glasgow–Liverpool/Manchester/Birmingham/Bristol. They also saw use on many freights on the ex-Caledonian line to Carlisle, as well as mail trains in and out of Central station. In addition, Class 81s were allocated to the mainly EMU depot at Shields Road for such workings.

The unreliability and non-standard nature of the early electric locomotives resulted in their gradual withdrawal from traffic between the late 1970s and the 1990s. The NBL-built 84s were the first to go, in 1980, while the last survivors were the Class 85s, which had seen increased freight employment. Anglo-Scottish Speedlink traffic from Mossend saw them stay in use until July 1991.

Class 86s (originally AL6) were far more successful. This much larger class was built later, in 1965–66, which allowed BR to combine the best features of the previous AL1–5 types in a new design. Reaching Glasgow Central regularly after 1974, the 86s saw regular passenger use on much of the same WCML expresses and freight traffic. They would become a regular sight over the years at Mossend Yard, and at the Freightliner depots at Coatbridge and Gushetfaulds, often working in pairs.

The BR TOPS system saw a continual and complex renumbering process over many years, with new 86 sub-classes created. This was mainly due to the gradual fitting of all locomotives with improved flexicoil suspension and new wheelsets, which allowed improved running speeds of up to 110mph. Eventually, most passenger workings were in the hands of the modified 86/1 and 86/2 series, while an 86/4 series was also later created by similar modifications to the remaining fleet. The 86/4s became dedicated to freight, surviving in traffic into the 1990s with Railfreight Distribution and appearing more and more often working in pairs. They were subsequently renumbered into a new 86/6 series, with Coatbridge-bound container trains becoming their main duty.

Passenger duties saw 86/2s and 86/4s continue to work regularly into Glasgow Central into the 1990s, first with the InterCity sector before most 86/2s passed over to Virgin Trains. These worked mainly Virgin CrossCountry services to destinations such as Birmingham, Bristol and Bournemouth, though they also appeared occasionally on some Euston expresses in lieu of Class 87s. No. 86245 was one particularly associated with Glasgow, being named *Caledonian* at

Glasgow Central in February 1998 and carrying a special 'Caledonian blue' version of the Virgin livery, albeit for just a year. The 86/4s were acquired by EWS, who used both them and 86/2s on postal traffic, first to Glasgow Central and then to the new Shieldmuir Royal Mail terminal, as well as sending them on hire to Virgin for the aforementioned passenger turns.

The EWS 86s were superseded by Class 67s and 90s at the turn of the millennium, while the Virgin fleet's days were numbered when Voyager units entered traffic. September 2002 saw all Virgin CrossCountry loco-hauled services go over to Class 220/221 haulage and mass withdrawals, though a few 86s survived helping out 87s on the Euston trains until the autumn of 2003. The only regular operator of the class in Scotland was then Freightliner, whose small fleet has defied the odds for years and continues to appear daily, working double-headed on lengthy intermodal trains between Coatbridge and Crewe/Tilbury. They have even started to gain Freightliner's elaborate new 'Powerhaul' livery, which looks slightly unusual on a 45+ year-old locomotive!

The Class 87 Electric Scots enjoyed a thirty-year stint as top link WCML express locomotives and rarely deviated from their designated Euston–Glasgow circuit throughout that time, though freight work such as intermodal trains could also produce them double-headed earlier in their career, and the unique thyristor-controlled 87101 was used by Railfreight Distribution in the 1990s (subsequently scrapped in 2002) while the rest of the class worked for InterCity.

After the introduction of DVTs in the early 1990s, Class 87s started to work Glasgow–Euston trains in push–pull mode out of Central station, with the locomotive usually at the Glasgow end of the train and the DVT at the other. After privatisation, Virgin operated the entire fleet until their final withdrawal in 2005, though they had ceased operating into Glasgow in October 2004. Pendolino EMUs had taken over their diagrams gradually from the early part of 2004.

Having brought in a train from the south, InterCity Executive-liveried 87007 *City of Manchester* stands at the buffers of Glasgow Central's platform 1, on 23 June 1990. (David Webster)

The Electric Scots (*c*.2003)

87001	*STEPHENSON*
87002	*Royal Sovereign*
87003	*Patriot*
87004	*Britannia*
87005	*City of London*
87006	*George Reynolds*
87007	*City of Manchester*
87008	*City of Liverpool*
87009	*City of Birmingham*
87010	*King Arthur*
87011	*City of Wolverhampton*
87012	*Coeur de Lion*
87013	*John O'Gaunt*
87014	*Knight of the Thistle*
87015	*Howard of Effingham*
87016	*Willesden Intercity Depot*
87017	*Iron Duke*
87018	*Lord Nelson*
87019	*Sir Winston Churchill*
87020	*North Briton*
87021	*Robert the Bruce*
87022	*Lew Adams The Black Prince*
87023	*Polmadie*
87024	*Lord of the Isles*
87025	*County of Cheshire*
87026	*Sir Richard Arkwright*
87027	*Wolf of Badenoch*
87028	*Lord President*
87029	*Earl Marischal*
87030	*Black Douglas*
87031	*Hal o' the Wynd*
87032	*Richard Fearn*
87033	*Thane of Fife*
87034	*William Shakespeare*
87035	*Robert Burns*

Three of the ex-Virgin 87s – 87006/22/8 – were released back into traffic in November 2004 by DRS, who intended to use them as new traction on their expanding Anglo-Scottish intermodal traffic, though they were withdrawn a short time later in favour of Class 66s. GBRf then hired four locomotives after putting Royal Mail postal traffic on the rails again, using them on a number of occasions to haul Class 325 units on trains to and from Shieldmuir terminal, mainly due to a shortage of 325 power cars. They were subsequently withdrawn in 2007. Aside from these limited appearances, one survivor has been the preserved BR blue-liveried 87002 *Royal Sovereign*, which has since visited Central station on railtour duties.

Class 90s were built by BREL at Crewe partly to supplement 87s on the Euston trains, entering traffic for the InterCity sector in 1989. Other machines went to Railfreight Distribution, where they held sway on a variety of freight workings in and out of Mossend and Coatbridge, including mixed Enterprises, intermodals and automotive workings, to destinations such as Warrington, Bescot and Wembley. Rail Express Systems, later superseded by EWS, used them on mail trains to Shieldmuir, while Freightliner locomotives would later be seen on the container and automotive flows.

Virgin still operated 90s on Glasgow–Euston services until Pendolino takeover in 2004, with EWS locomotives also hired in for these workings. However, one duty in and out of Glasgow Central which the 90s have retained through the years is the Glasgow–Euston sleeper train, now known as the Caledonian Sleeper 'Lowland' service. Locomotives are hired in from DB Schenker (formerly EWS) for this purpose, with 90019/20/4 currently painted in First ScotRail 'Barbie' livery as part of the contract. In addition, Freightliner and DB Schenker locomotives still cover a varied range of freight turns out of Mossend and Coatbridge.

Class 91s first graced the platforms of Glasgow Central on 30 May 1991, when some of the East Coast Main Line InterCity 225 express services were extended to run from Edinburgh to Glasgow over the newly electrified line via Carstairs (traversing the WCML through Motherwell). The ECML itself had gone 'under the wires' the previous year. The new Glasgow–London King's Cross workings would use InterCity 225 rakes, comprising a 91 (at the Glasgow end) and a DVT sandwiching Mark 4 coaches, and offering a service to rival the more familiar West Coast route.

The InterCity 225s would become an everyday sight at Central for many years after this, continuing in use under GNER, who operated a Monday–Saturday timetable with arrivals and departures roughly every two hours. However, the Glasgow–King's Cross service was eventually cut down to just one train a day in each direction under new franchise East Coast Trains (taking over from National Express East Coast), currently the 0650 ex-Glasgow and 1530 ex-King's Cross services.

Virgin still offer a faster alternative service to the British capital, while CrossCountry still operate from Glasgow to Edinburgh via Carstairs using Voyagers.

The supreme haulage capabilities of Class 87s and 90s are bettered by Class 92s, which have a mammoth tractive effort of 90,000lbf, allowing them to tackle the steep gradients of the West Coast Main Line with ease. Though very reliable and popular with crews, the class have a history of being very under-utilised as it was never made possible to use them on their intended work, which was the operation of long-distance freight and overnight passenger services the whole way from Glasgow/Edinburgh to France via the Channel Tunnel. As a result, the 92s have ended up being used on many types of traffic they were not intended for. A regular diagram in the early 2000s was EWS's 4M63/4S61 return Mossend–Warrington Arpley timber train, while they also became regulars working the daily Mossend–Carlisle Enterprise. Heavy international freights between Mossend and Wembley or Dollands Moor have long been solid diagrams for the class too and these are at least more in keeping with the sort of work they were designed for.

Mossend Yard remains the key place to see 92s in action in Glasgow, where they are stabled between working Enterprise and intermodal workings to Bescot, Doncaster and Trafford Park amongst others. Formerly used over the WCML as part of the Railfreight Distribution pool, they are now mostly owned by DB Schenker, though a few of GBRf's new fleet have also started to reach Scotland. Then there is DRS, which has been hiring DB locomotives, as the company finally realises its quest to use electric traction on Anglo-Scottish intermodal traffic. Their use has been a prelude to the introduction of Vossloh dual-mode Class 88s.

Electric multiple units

The Class 303 'Blue Trains' became very much a Glasgow institution over the years. They are fondly remembered by not only rail enthusiasts, but also by members of the general public, who, after their grand launch in 1960, immediately took a liking to the units' state-of-the-art design and took to the rails. Especially worthy of note were the air-operated sliding doors and plush, spacious interiors that were well ahead of their time. Not just that, but the 303s were a class indigenous to Glasgow, being built by nearby Pressed Steel of Linwood and, except for a period in the 1980s when a dozen or so units worked in north-west England, all of them spent their entire career around the Glasgow and Inverclyde area.

It was the imaginative 'Caledonian blue' colour scheme the 303s were delivered in that gave them their famous nickname, but unfortunately this was short-lived, with all examples repainted into the darker BR 'corporate blue' colours in the late 1960s. This would in turn be replaced by BR blue and grey in the late 1970s.

The electrified North Clyde route from Balloch/Helensburgh/Milngavie to Springburn/Airdrie remained their domain until Class 320 introduction in 1990, as well as Neilston and Newton workings via the Cathcart Circle. The electrification of the Hamilton Circle and Lanark branch saw the 303s become regulars there too, together with the Clyde coast routes which took them to Gourock, Wemyss Bay and Largs.

The introduction of Class 314s, 318s then 320s, and the withdrawal of the 311s, would see the 303s work more and more varied diagrams, becoming more common for example on the Argyle line and to Gourock and Wemyss Bay. Refurbishment of most units also took place in the 1980s and this would see a solid wall placed between the driving car saloons and the driver's cab, which replaced the glass screen that formerly gave passengers a driver's-eye view similar to many DMU types. The new look 303s also gained Strathclyde PTE orange and black livery and had their old two-character headcode panels plated over, with high-intensity headlights added from 1990. It was also notable by now that the units had their initial wrap-around front windscreens cut back to the cab fronts. This change resulted from a tragic incident in 1974 that saw a driver killed by a missile thrown at a train near Garrowhill.

The first 303 to be withdrawn, back in 1981, was 303035; the one member of the class which was experimentally fitted with thyristor control and 'plug' automatic doors. Accidents also saw several of the class written off. No. 303051 was of course one such example, being the unit that ran away from Westerton and collided with 37011 on 30 January 1987. No. 303091 was involved in a collision with a DMU at Gower Street, outside Glasgow Central, on 30 September 1973, in which the driver and four passengers died, with fifty others injured, though in this instance the unit was subsequently repaired and reinstated. There were also a number of withdrawals of un-refurbished 303s in the late 1980s after asbestos was discovered and Class 320s arrived on the scene.

Those who regularly travelled past Shields Road on passing trains during the 1990s may recall a 303 painted in original 'Caledonian blue' livery which often sat in the sidings. The unit in question was the un-refurbished 303048, which received the heritage repaint at BRML Springburn in 1991 and was used over the next few years on various private charters. It was also used by ScotRail on service trains over the Inverclyde lines. Although it had originally been planned to preserve one of the driving cars (BDTSO No. 75808) at the Glasgow Museum of Transport, asbestos content prevented this and saw the unit scrapped in 1998.

The 1990s saw the 303s cover much of the same varied route pattern around Glasgow and four examples (303019/21/3/87) gained new SPT carmine and cream livery from 1997. However, the decision by ScotRail to rid itself of any trains built prior to 1970 would mean the end of the line for the class and so withdrawals started to mount. A handful of examples would manage to soldier on for longer than expected into the new millennium, due to problems with their replacements, the new Class 334s, but the end was nigh.

ScotRail gave the 42-year-old electrics a suitable send-off on 30 December 2002, when 303011/88 formed the class' last ever working on the 0927 Bellgrove–Helensburgh Central service. The units were greeted by a piper on the platform and adorned with a special wreath upon arrival at Helensburgh, with large crowds out to pay their final respects to the 'Blue Trains'. No. 303032 would live on in preservation at the Bo'ness and Kinneil Railway, being the only survivor of this much-loved EMU class.

The Class 311s were close relatives of the 303s, built by Cravens of Sheffield, and numbered nineteen three-car sets in total. Built in 1967, they were constructed to very much the same design specifications as the 303s and externally they looked almost identical, though the 311s had more powerful traction motors. They were also built solely for use on the Gourock and Wemyss Bay routes, but they soon saw use on the city low-level lines too. All carried plain BR dark blue and full yellow warning panels from new, unlike the iconic 'Caledonian blue' seen on the 303s, before receiving the blue and grey standard coaching stock livery in the late 1970s. Units 311092/9/109 would subsequently carry Strathclyde PTE orange and black from the mid 1980s, adding further to the confusion between them and the 303s!

The 311s had their wrap-around windscreens shortened and headcode panels replaced with a 'domino' display in the 1970s, the same as their Scottish-built sisters, but this would be the extent of modifications on the class. Despite being newer than the 303s, they started to be withdrawn in the late 1980s, with the arrival of Class 318s and 320s proving to be their death knell. November 1990 saw the last few 311s withdrawn from passenger service, though two of them, 311103/4, would survive in use as sandite units based at Shields Road depot.

The sandite units were eventually given the departmental numbers of 936103/4 and repainted in Railtrack gold, white and grey colours, though they only lasted until 1999 when they were retired from service. No. 936103 (311103) would pass into preservation and became based at Summerlee Heritage Park in Coatbridge, placed on static display on a section of track in the outdoor section of the museum and eventually repainted back into plain BR blue, but without numbers or logos. Unfortunately, its condition has since deteriorated and it was reduced to just two cars when one of the driving-trailers was sold and scrapped.

The sixteen York-built Class 314 three-car units were built for use on the newly-reopened Argyle line via Glasgow Central low-level opening in 1979 and survive today as the oldest multiple units in the ScotRail fleet. Like most of the other electrics in the fleet, their routes varied over the years and it was no surprise that they ended up working many North Clyde turns alongside Classes 303 and

Class 314 No. 314207 pulls into Mount Florida with the 1432 Cathcart–Glasgow Central on 18 January 2014. This is essentially a Cathcart Inner Circle service which left Glasgow Central at 1415. (Author's collection)

320 into the 1990s. Their initial BR blue and grey was swapped in the 1980s for Strathclyde orange, before SPT carmine and cream (or 'blood and custard') took hold in the late 1990s.

As with the other units, they would migrate to other lines when older types were withdrawn or new ones introduced. Class 334 introduction and 303 withdrawal resulted in more sweeping changes around 1999, when the 314s became virtually extinct on the Argyle line and moved instead to the Cathcart Circle, operating from Glasgow Central high-level to Neilston and Newton. They would go on to dominate this route for some time and were ideal for cobbling together on football specials running to Mount Florida. They also began appearing regularly on Glasgow–Gourock/Wemyss Bay services, though this has been restricted in more recent years to mostly weekend and peak-time workings.

At the time of going to press, Class 314s are still in regular use on Cathcart, Neilston and Newton diagrams, as well as most Sunday services to Wemyss Bay and other peak-time Inverclyde workings. They also gained new track in 2012 when the Paisley Canal line went electric. After speculation of imminent withdrawal, ScotRail have pledged to stick with the class in the short-term and a life extension programme has seen all units recently refurbished at Springburn works, which is likely to be the last overhaul they will ever get. A handful of the units have so far also received ScotRail Saltire livery as part of this, as well as having their interiors spruced up with new seat covers, breathing new life into their old design. But given that the 314s may not be around for much longer, the message for photographers is catch them while you can!

Also built by BREL in York, and an indigenous Scottish type, are the Class 318s. Twenty-one three-car units were built in 1986 for use on Glasgow Central–Ayr/ Ardrossan/Largs services after those lines were electrified. This became their stamping ground throughout the 1990s, before the 2002 introduction of Class 334s saw them gradually displaced from these duties and transferred instead to the Glasgow low-level system. This saw them starting to be used mainly on services from Milngavie/Dalmuir to Motherwell/Lanark. Gourock and Wemyss Bay also saw more regular 318 action alongside the other varying types of EMUs.

A major change for the 90mph-capable 318s came in late 2005, when they started to be overhauled by Hunslet-Barclay of Kilmarnock. As well as interior

A Saltire-liveried Class 320 crosses Coatdyke Viaduct, near Airdrie, with a service for Balloch on 11 January 2014. (Author's collection)

refurbishment, including improved toilet facilities, all units had their cab end gangway connections removed to give a virtually flush front with an extra window added. Not only did this alter their external appearance, but it gave drivers a much improved view.

Class 318s were displaced from regular duties on the Ayrshire and Inverclyde routes during 2011 and became thereafter solely concentrated on the city low-level lines. They now run regularly in multiple with Class 320s and are in the process of being re-liveried from SPT carmine and cream into ScotRail Saltire colours (or 'Spotrail' as it is known to enthusiasts!).

An attractive feature of the later-built Class 320s, introduced on the North Clyde line in 1990, is the murals painted on the walls of their saloons by the Glasgow School of Art, featuring well-known Clydeside landmarks such as the Kelvingrove Art Gallery and Wemyss Bay station. This was just a small part of a £30 million investment by Strathclyde PTE to have these three-car units constructed by BREL in York. The twenty-two-strong class would go on to establish themselves permanently on the Balloch/Milngavie–Springburn/Airdrie/Drumgelloch circuit, though their distinctive whine is now heard regularly on the Argyle line too. The opening of the Airdrie–Bathgate link in 2011 saw the cascade of more 334s to North Clyde workings; hence the reallocation of many 320s to Dalmuir/Milngavie–Motherwell/Lanark/Larkhall diagrams, marking the first time they had ever regularly strayed from the Queen Street route.

The 320s were the first Strathclyde units to be built for driver-only operation, though delays in the new procedures meant that they still used a guard for giving the 'right away' during station stops in their early days. An initial dispute related to this resulted in an overtime ban for guards and more than 300 services being cancelled over a three-day period during 1990. Other new design features on the units included dot-matrix destination boards, which were later replaced by

Class 320s: Previous names carried

320305	GLASGOW SCHOOL OF ART 1844-150-1994
320306	Model Rail Scotland
320308	High Road 20th Anniversary 2000
320309	Radio Clyde 25th Anniversary
320311	Royal College of Physicians and Surgeons of Glasgow
320312	Sir William A Smith, Founder of the Boys Brigade
320321	The Rt. Hon. John Smith, QC, MP
320322	Festive Glasgow Orchid

bright LED types in common with other classes used in Strathclyde. The electrics controlling their automatic doors are said to be resistant to temperatures of as low as -19°C, which would have been tested during the 'Big Freezes' of 2009 and 2010.

The Class 320s also carried a number of Scottish-themed names whilst used by SPT, including *Model Rail Scotland*, the name given to the large annual model railway exhibition which has been a regular feature at Glasgow's SECC arena for many years. These have since been removed as the 320s have been repainted from carmine and cream into Saltire livery.

Externally similar to Class 320s, ScotRail previously had the whole fleet of four-car Class 322s (322481–85) on loan to provide a solution for Edinburgh–North Berwick workings during two different spells between 2001 and 2011. ScotRail also utilised them on two daily through-services each way from Glasgow Central–North Berwick, running via Carstairs. Initially, the five units were leased from West Anglia Great Northern, with most still painted in white Stansted Express livery, though 322484 carried blue First North Western. No. 322485 received the name *North Berwick Flyer 1850–2000*.

The cessation of this contract saw the 322s transferred south again during summer 2004, but the next year they were leased again and based once more at Shields Road depot for the same workings. This time, the whole fleet was painted in First ScotRail 'Barbie' colours, with 322481 taking the *North Berwick Flyer* name from 322485. In 2011 the 322s had their second long holiday north of the border come to an end with the introduction of Class 380s on the North Berwick branch, and they would subsequently begin a new life with Northern Rail.

Class 325 postal units were regular visitors to Glasgow Central and thereafter Shieldmuir Royal Mail terminal when it took over as the railhead for mail trains in the city. Taking over some traffic from loco-hauled sets, they worked daily for EWS between Shieldmuir and Willesden, London, via the WCML until 2003 saw Royal Mail cease to use rail transport. After being made redundant for a period, GBRf gained a new rail contract with the company for Christmas 2004 and brought the units back to Shieldmuir.

In 2010 EWS, by then taken over by DB Schenker, regained the mail contract and they continue to employ 325s on one train in each direction per day between Shieldmuir and Willesden. As in the past, the 325s normally work these in multiple, usually three four-car sets together. There continue to be extra workings in the run-up to Christmas.

The Class 334 Junipers form another part of ScotRail's vast EMU fleet and, like most other classes, they have been redeployed on routes which they were never originally intended for. Originally built for SPT to work Glasgow–Gourock/Wemyss Bay/Largs/Ardrossan/Ayr services, and marking the biggest investment of new trains in Strathclyde since the 'Blue Trains' were launched in 1960, a full introduction of the forty units was heavily delayed as the class suffered from a number of initial technical faults. Pioneer unit 334001 was delivered to Scotland on 2 August 1999, with the intention that all would be in service by May 2000. It was only after countless modifications and driver training runs that all 334s were finally able to enter traffic in December 2002.

The Junipers offered the public many exciting modern features, including spacious, high-backed seating, an automatic public address system with digital monitors which announced all station stops, and interior saloons at near-platform-level height which meant less of a 'jump' for boarding passengers. They were all three-car units and soon became a regular sight on the North Clyde and Argyle lines (essentially most Glasgow low-level services in the period *c.* 2003–11 were a toss-up between Classes 318/320/334!) as well as at Glasgow Central high-level. Glasgow–Ayr workings, especially during peak hours, usually employed six-car formations while the rest tended to be three cars.

A big transformation occurred with the reopening of the line from Glasgow to Edinburgh via Airdrie and Bathgate in December 2010. All Class 334s were gradually cascaded on to the new Helensburgh Central–Edinburgh workings in

The first public service out of Glasgow Central using Class 350 Desiro EMUs took place on a very wet 30 December 2013, when unbranded grey units 350403/401 worked the 1109 service to Manchester Piccadily. Here they are captured speeding through Cambuslang. (Author's collection)

early 2011, giving all their turns on the Ayrshire and Clyde coast routes over to Class 380s. Today, the Edinburgh trains are their main duty, usually worked in six-car formations, though they also appear on other North Clyde services such as Dalmuir–Springburn. The units are now uncommon on the Argyle line and rarer still at Glasgow Central high-level.

Siemens Desiro Class 350 EMUs are a far less familiar type, which have only recently started operation in Scotland. First TransPennine Express is currently introducing a fleet of ten (sub-class 350/4 Nos 350401–10) to replace most Class 185s between Glasgow Central and Manchester Airport/Manchester Piccadilly, making logical use of the electric wires on the WCML. All are brand-new units, built in 2013–14, and operate as four-car sets, though they can be combined to eight cars.

Class 380s joined the ScotRail fleet in 2010, primarily for all Ayrshire and Inverclyde services originating at Glasgow Central, though they were initially ordered for use on the Glasgow Airport Rail Link before it was abolished. There are currently thirty-eight sets all in all; twenty-two three-car (380/0) and sixteen four-car (380/1), all of which were introduced into traffic gradually from December 2010 to summer 2011. Similar to the 334s, their introduction was delayed by teething problems, specifically software faults, which resulted in knock-on stock shortages.

Class 380s have worked some turns over the Paisley Canal branch since electrification, in addition to booked diagrams from Glasgow Central to Gourock/Wemyss Bay/Largs/Ardrossan/Ayr. Table seats, air conditioning and onboard power sockets are amongst the advantages they offer over the previously-used 334s. Wi-fi will also be made available during 2014.

BR had once predicted that by 1978, Advanced Passenger Trains (APTs) would be in everyday revenue-earning service over the West Coast Main Line from London to Glasgow. While this never quite happened, the Class 370 APT-P prototypes went through an extensive period of testing on the northern section of the line during the early 1980s, being based for some time at Shields Road depot. A few special publicity runs also saw unit 370005 operate over the Glasgow suburban network, including a trip westwards to Hyndland via Exhibition Centre for the opening of the SECC arena. There was also famously a new all-time speed record set on 12 September 1984 between London Euston and Glasgow, with an APT completing the northbound journey in three hours fifty-two minutes and the southbound in four hours fourteen minutes. Yet, the units were plagued with problems throughout their testing period and all were withdrawn by 1986.

Far more successful tilting trains than the APTs, the Class 390 Pendolinos carried high-speed Anglo-Scottish travel to new heights when they took over Virgin West Coast passenger duties from Class 87s and 90s. An all-time high-speed record was set for the southbound Glasgow–London journey on 22 September 2006, when 390047 *Heaven's Angel* completed it, non-stop, in three hours fifty-five minutes, bettering the APT's southbound record twenty-two years earlier.

Originally, Virgin had fifty-three Pendolinos with nine-car sets being the norm, until 2009 saw four new eleven-car sets added to the fleet. With extra vehicles subsequently added to other sets, thirty-five of the class now run as eleven cars (classified 390/1), with the other twenty-two (390/0) still nine cars. No. 390033 received the name *City of Glasgow* at Central station on 21 May 2004, but was subsequently written off after being involved in the Grayrigg accident on 23 February 2007. Coincidentally, this name was originally carried by LMS 'Duchess' Pacific No. 46242, which itself was badly damaged in the 1952 Harrow derailment.

8

Passenger Traffic

North Clyde/Argyle lines

The elimination of steam in BR's Scottish Region during the 1960s and the introduction of diesel and electric services brought with it a new era of clockface timetabling, meaning that most trains would arrive and depart from each station at the same regular intervals every hour throughout the day. Under steam, arrival and departure times had followed a more irregular and unpredictable pattern, which could be a headache for the average passenger.

Class 334 No. 334021 emerges from the darkness at Charing Cross with the 1848 Edinburgh–Helensburgh Central, as 318253 enters the long tunnel towards Queen Street low-level on the 1723 Balloch–Airdrie, on 11 January 2014. (Author's collection)

The new system was most apparent on the shorter-distance suburban services, starting with the introduction of the 'Blue Trains' in Glasgow, where BR was quick to point out the faster journey times on offer compared to steam haulage. From Helensburgh Central to Glasgow Queen Street low-level, the Class 303s took fifty-one minutes; steam took sixty-four minutes. The half-hourly frequency between Helensburgh and Airdrie from that period continued right through the decades (today the workings are extended through to Edinburgh), with naturally a few extra peak-hour diagrams too. The 'Blue Train' timetable also had the generous offering of half-hourly workings over this section throughout most of the day on a Sunday, another feature that remains today.

Also notable from some of the earlier timetables was the inclusion of two-digit headcode numbers which allowed passengers to identify their train, much like bus services. A '15', for example, denoted an Airdrie working while a '65' was for Springburn. Ever since the 1960s, Springburn and Balloch have generally continued to be served on a half-hourly basis on the North Clyde line, as Bridgeton Central was before it closed. One major change in May 2014 will see the half-hourly Dalmuir–Springburn service extended through to Cumbernauld, after the Springburn–Cumbernauld route is electrified.

Milngavie was generally always served by a half-hourly North Clyde service, though it eventually had its frequency doubled after the 2005 opening of the Larkhall branch. Today, there are two trains an hour from there to Edinburgh, plus one to Motherwell and one to Lanark along the Argyle line. Airdrie, on the other hand, had four trains per hour in each direction after the opening of Drumgelloch terminus (two of these continued on to Drumgelloch) and now enjoys no less than six for most of the day, with four being through workings to and from Edinburgh.

Traffic over the Argyle line was heavy just after reopening in 1979, with seven trains each way per hour. The 1982–83 timetable shows two from Dumbarton Central to Motherwell (one via Bellshill, one via Hamilton), two Dalmuir–Motherwell via Hamilton, two Dalmuir–Motherwell via Bellshill and one limited stop from Anderston to Lanark. However, this would not last. Fast-forward twenty years and it was down to just four per hour; three Dalmuir–Motherwell and one Dalmuir–Lanark. This lasted until Larkhall services began in 2005, when it went back up to six an hour. For a number of years there has also been a few trains to Motherwell extended through to Coatbridge Central in the morning and evening peaks.

One long-standing oddity from the Argyle line timetable which survives to this day is a Monday–Friday teatime service out to Carstairs; for some time this has been the only train on the route which travels any further south than Lanark. Now it runs as the 1701 Dalmuir–Carstairs, with a return 0806 Carstairs–Garscadden in the morning. Both are run for the benefit of commuters in Lanarkshire.

In addition, ScotRail also introduced a new Monday–Saturday electric service from Glasgow Central high-level to Edinburgh Waverley via Carstairs in December 2012, taking the same route as the two trains each way from Glasgow to North Berwick.

The North Clyde and Argyle lines have seen a good mixture of different EMU types in regular use since the 1980s and today there is still plenty of variety, with classes 318, 320 and 334 all in daily use. Their SPT and ScotRail liveries are now up-to-date with European Union disabled access rules brought in after the millennium, which state that doors must be more distinctively coloured to help partially sighted people identify them more easily.

In terms of the passengers themselves, trains along the low-level routes are mainly dominated by commuters, while there are considerable flows of shoppers and night-time revellers at weekends. Those to and from Exhibition Centre station are often packed with concert-goers too, while Bellgrove and Dalmarnock are heavily used by football fans travelling to Celtic Park. The changes in fare prices through the years also makes for interesting reading. In 1981, a day single from Helensburgh to Lanark cost just £2.94, while Hyndland to Finnieston was a mere 27 pence!

North suburban

Following Beeching and the cessation of many local services, such as Glasgow–Kirkintilloch, the stations of Bishopbriggs, Croy and Lenzie would thereafter be served mainly by half-hourly 'stoppers' from Glasgow Queen Street to Falkirk Grahamston or Dunblane. Today it is a half-hourly service to Alloa and half-hourly to Stirling, while Falkirk Grahamston is now reached via Stepps and Cumbernauld.

In recent years, there have been two DMUs per hour calling at all stations from Glasgow Queen Street to Cumbernauld, one of these extending to Falkirk Grahamston, plus the hourly Motherwell–Cumbernauld shuttle. However, at the time of writing, electrification of the Cumbernauld line is imminent and this will see both the Motherwell and Glasgow–Cumbernauld services taken over by EMUs on the low-level system. The Glasgow–Falkirk Grahamston workings will remain DMU-operated out of Queen Street high-level.

Services from Queen Street high-level to Maryhill/Anniesland have, by and large, stuck to a half-hourly formula through the years, with classes 156, 158, and 170 all seeing use. There are currently no scheduled Sunday trains on the Maryhill line, though recent years have seen ScotRail run a special hourly service from Anniesland during the Christmas shopping season. The same system has also been used on other routes, such as to Paisley Canal and Whifflet.

South suburban

The doomed Kilmacolm branch had an hourly DMU running right up until its closure in 1983, with no Sunday service. Most ran via Paisley Canal and Crookston, but there was also a morning peak working each way that took the Paisley Gilmour Street route. Today's Paisley Canal electric service is half-hourly and Monday–Saturday only.

East Kilbride's service from Glasgow Central is also half-hourly and has been since the inaugural Sprinter timetable of October 1988. Prior to this, services had been roughly one per hour since Beeching, including a few peak-time fast trains that did not call at all stations en route. Barrhead, on the other hand, had a DMU terminating service from Glasgow running every two hours, which actually rose to every hour following Beeching. Most Glasgow–Kilmarnock locals also stopped here, though these ran irregularly, with Glasgow–Carlisle loco-hauled services also calling at Kilmarnock. The Glasgow–Kilmarnocks became hourly after going over to Sprinters in 1989, then half-hourly in 2009 when double track was installed between Lugton and Stewarton.

Clockface departures on the East Kilbride line mean that, if running to time, Sprinters pass every half-hour at Clarkston. On 28 November 2013, 156512 departs for East Kilbride bang on time at 10.07 a.m., as classmate 156506 sits with the corresponding working to Glasgow Central. (Author's collection)

1967: Price Of Second-Class Day Return to and from Glasgow Central

	s/d
Airdrie	3/10
Clydebank Central	2/1
East Kilbride	3/9
Neilston	3/2
Newton	2/8
Paisley Canal/Gilmour Street	2/6
Pollokshaws West	1/7

The Cathcart Circle and its connecting lines to Neilston and Newton have all been grouped together on the same timetable since 'Blue Train' operations started in 1962. The frequency implemented back then – comprising no less than ten trains an hour from Glasgow Central – continued throughout the 1970s. The ten services were: two Cathcart Inner Circle, two Cathcart Outer Circle, two Glasgow–Neilston via Mount Florida, two Glasgow–Newton via Mount Florida and two Glasgow–Kirkhill via Maxwell Park. Certain Newton services would also continue on to Motherwell.

Local services operated between Glasgow Central high-level and Motherwell prior to the reopening of the Central low-level line in 1979. Here we see a 'Blue Train' stopping at the erstwhile WCML platforms at Rutherglen in October 1975. (Allan Trotter, Eastbank Model Railway Club)

Today, the same destinations are served on the Cathcart Circle every hour, but with reduced frequencies: one Cathcart Inner, one Cathcart Outer, two Glasgow–Neilston via Mount Florida, one Glasgow-Newton via Mount Florida and one Glasgow–Newton via Maxwell Park, with a higher frequency at peak times. This is still an adequate service by anyone's standards and, if anything, the decrease on the western side of the circle has been outweighed by the dramatic increase on the neighbouring GSWR main line, which serves some of the same area. Shawlands and Pollokshaws East's half-hourly electric service, for example, is complemented by Sprinters stopping at Pollokshaws West every 10–20 minutes to and from Glasgow Central; and with most stops on the Cathcart Circle around half a mile from each other, every resident in the immediate south side district has a station within spitting distance.

Inverclyde and Ayrshire

Class 303 and 311 EMUs established a more frequent service on the Glasgow Central-Greenock-Gourock Clyde coast route, which still connects with Gourock-Dunoon/Kilcreggan ferry services. A basic pattern of three trains an hour in each direction has long been the norm, with a few extras during peak hours too, but May 2014 will see it rise to four per hour. There will now be two limited-stop 'fast' services every hour compared to the previous one, taking thirty-nine minutes each way, plus the two existing 'slow' trains which take around an hour. It is noteworthy that until the regular use of Class 334s started in 2001, passengers usually had to contend with no toilet for this lengthy journey. Glasgow-Wemyss Bay meanwhile, has an hourly service that goes back decades.

Glasgow–Ayr services started running to a new half-hourly clockface timetable in the 1960s with Swindon Cross-Country DMUs. Today's Monday-Friday electric service is four trains each way per hour, the fourth train being a recent addition which formerly only went from Glasgow to Irvine, and with a few workings even now extending as through-services from Edinburgh and North Berwick via Carstairs (albeit with reversal at Glasgow Central). Even well before the introduction of Class 380s, six-car trains or longer were commonplace, especially at rush hours. Capacity is also required for passengers to Prestwick Airport, plus the annual Gold Cup event at Ayr Racecourse held in mid September. Beeching and the end of steam brought an end to the many race specials that used to run, as well as holiday trains between Glasgow and Heads of Ayr.

Glasgow Central–Stranraer workings used to be one part of the public's main travel link from Scotland to Northern Ireland, connecting with car ferries to Larne and Belfast at Stranraer Harbour. After reverting from DMUs back to loco-haulage, the 1984 introduction of Class 47/4s with Electric Train Heating saw faster and more reliable services, while a rake of dual-heat Mark 1 coaches were repainted in a colourful red, blue and white livery with 'Sealink' branding for use on the boat trains. The 1988 introduction of Class 156 Sprinters saw shorter trains, though passenger loadings remained healthy until 2011, when ferry services were drastically moved from Stranraer Harbour to nearby Cairnryan, thereby ending all direct train–boat connections. As a result, it is possible that the remaining service of three trains a day between Glasgow and Stranraer could be lost too under the next ScotRail franchise.

Glasgow–Ardrossan Harbour services have also long provided a train–ferry connection, albeit with Caledonian MacBrayne running to Arran. Passengers from Glasgow to Largs can also still catch a boat to Millport, though this involves a little walking distance as well.

Edinburgh and the north

Passengers travelling from Glasgow to Edinburgh are now spoilt for choice, with services along four different routes; something probably difficult to imagine back in the 1960s, when it would have been cut to just one if Beeching's proposal to close the Shotts route had gone ahead. Despite the reopening of Airdrie–Bathgate, it is the original main line from Glasgow Queen Street via Polmont which remains the most prestigious of the four. Schedules on the latter have always been designed with high speed in mind, while the ex-Caledonian line via Shotts was always about providing a link between the city and the small communities of Lanarkshire and West Lothian. Journey times on the main route have historically been much longer than they are now, and gradually shortened through the years. In 1967, the quickest journey time under Class 126 DMUs was fifty-five minutes from Edinburgh and an hour from Glasgow Queen Street, while the Shotts route took one hour twenty-six minutes from Edinburgh and one hour twenty-one minutes from Glasgow Central.

It is worth noting that the Shotts services stopped at nearly all stations en route along their 46½-mile journey. Carfin was originally omitted except for morning workings but now all stopping trains call here. Additionally, during the 1980s there were a few early morning and evening services which started or terminated at Hamilton West instead of Glasgow Central. Trains along the route today are half-hourly (they were formerly hourly), with every second one being an express, calling at Bellshill only in the Glasgow area.

The Edinburgh and Glasgow main line has gradually seen services speeded up at the same time as improvements have been made to its main competitor, the M8 motorway (which has subsequently suffered more and more from congestion). The half-hourly frequency under Class 27s continued with the

Class 47/7s, though stops at Bishopbriggs, Lenzie and Croy were gradually weeded out on most services to tighten schedules. The best journey times of 43–44 minutes were also stretched out to mostly 48 minutes by the late 1980s. In September 1999, they would go up to their present-day fifteen-minute frequency, following the opening of Cowlairs Signalling Centre and the introduction of Class 170 Turbostars.

In 1970, the Town Clerk in Stirling wrote a letter to BR management in dismay at the lack of local services between the town and Glasgow, questioning the lack of improvements at a time when the Edinburgh–Glasgow route was receiving enhancements to its services. It also criticised the late running of many longer-distance services that called there from Inverness, Dundee and Aberdeen.

The hourly Glasgow–Aberdeen expresses of today were formerly every two hours under push–pull 47/7s. Like the Glasgow–Edinburghs of that era, air-conditioned Mark 2 coaches were used (usually one first-class in each rake), though during the final few years they were largely replaced by the newer Mark 3s, some in Intercity 'red stripe' livery instead of ScotRail 'blue stripe'. The Edinburgh formations normally had the locomotive leading out of Glasgow and the DBSO push–pull unit at the other end, whilst on the Aberdeen workings it was more unpredictable. May 1990 saw the end of loco-haulage, with Class 156 Sprinters having to be used on some Edinburgh and Aberdeen services until October due to the unavailability of new 158s.

Routes towards the Highlands have always had a much sparser direct service from Glasgow. The Inverness trains of course started using Queen Street station as their terminus after Buchanan Street closed in 1966, with generally three to four trains a day during the loco-hauled era. Latterly, 47/4s hauling five-coach rakes of Mark 2s (including a micro-buffet) were the norm and there was also an overnight sleeper between Glasgow/Edinburgh and Inverness. The frequency has fluctuated since the use of 158s and 170s, with many workings from Glasgow to Perth only and changes available on to Edinburgh–Inverness services; but as of the December 2013 timetable change, there are now five Down and four Up Glasgow–Inverness services.

On the West Highland routes, Glasgow–Oban has generally been three trains a day for most of the years since Beeching, while Glasgow–Fort William was the same until Sprinters were introduced in 1989. This saw most trains to Oban and Fort William combined to run as part of the same service to Crianlarich, with four of these each way per day as well as the London Euston–Fort William sleeper. In October 1993, they both went back to three a day, plus the sleeper. Some services still run combined to Crianlarich, especially during the winter months, while Fort William trains now run as through-services to Mallaig. May 2014 will see a big change, when the Glasgow–Oban service is doubled to six trains per day.

The Fort William–Euston Caledonian Sleeper takes an unusual route each night between Westerton and Greenhill Junction, near Falkirk, which sees it travel through the north and west Glasgow suburbs. The early morning Down working takes the line to Cowlairs via Cumbernauld and thereafter towards Maryhill. However, the Up train leaves Maryhill and traverses the 140yd section between Cowlairs North and Cowlairs East junctions, and on to the Edinburgh and Glasgow main line. It is the only train to use that particular Cowlairs East Curve regularly and following the service's threatened withdrawal in May 1995,

Westerton: the sleeper connection

As dawn breaks on the early spring morning of 21 March 2012, 156465 rolls into Westerton at 5.43 a.m., with the 0530 service from Glasgow Queen Street high-level. This working is provided specifically to connect with the Caledonian Sleeper to Fort William. (Author's collection)

Ten minutes later, Class 67 No. 67007 arrives with the 0450 Edinburgh–Fort William portion of the sleeper from London Euston. Though empty for now, the station's platforms will soon be filled with commuters as the first of the day's electric service trains begin. (Author's collection)

a 2359 Bishopbriggs–Maryhill local was introduced for a short period, a 'ghost train' run only as a means to justify keeping that section of line open.

One far more useful local working, which is in the current timetable, is the early morning 0530 Glasgow Queen Street–Westerton, which runs Monday–Saturday to allow a city centre connection with the Fort William sleeper. It returns each night on weekdays as the 0005 Westerton–Queen Street (2328 on Sundays). After arrival at Westerton, the morning train now runs empty stock to Arrochar and Tarbet on the West Highland Line to form the 0710 Arrochar–Glasgow Queen Street commuter service via Maryhill.

Anglo-Scottish

The Glasgow Central–Carlisle via Dumfries service has been roughly one train every two to three hours for the past few decades. As on the Stranraer line, Mark 1 carriages still made up most trains right up until 3 October 1988, when they became mostly two-car Sprinters instead. Long before this – back in 1967 – most were Anglo-Scottish services, such as the Thames–Clyde Express. Its Up working departed Glasgow Central at 0940 with the Down arriving at 1905. There was also a daily express that arrived at Central from Leeds City at 1510 and departed south at 1605, plus two overnight sleepers to London: the 2125 to St Pancras and the 2210 limited-stop to Euston via Kilmarnock. Both daytime trains had a restaurant car, offering dinner for the minimum price of 13s 6d.

One major undertaking in the run-up to West Coast Main Line electrification was the replacement of Cook Street underbridge on the approach to Glasgow Central station, between 22 and 31 July 1973. During this period, a number of trains were diverted over the GSWR main line via Paisley Gilmour Street and Dalry. The location of the bridge repairs meant that existing service trains booked to run from Kilmarnock to Glasgow via Barrhead had either to take the Dalry line or to be routed to Shields Junction for reversal. Several early morning parcels trains were sent either via Paisley Canal or the Cathcart Circle, before a reversal at Shields.

During these diversions, both overnight sleeping-car expresses that were normally routed via the WCML from London Euston to Glasgow Central (1S13 and 1S18) went via Kilmarnock and Paisley, along with the Euston–Perth sleeper (1S25), which still ran at this time. Complementing these were the two sleepers that had a regular booked path via the GSWR line (1S24 from St Pancras and 1S26 from Euston). Southbound highlights, as well as several Glasgow–Euston expresses, included the 1M27 0830 Glasgow–Liverpool Lime Street, the Saturdays-only 1M21 0837 to Blackpool and 1M32 0857 to Morecambe, and 1M47 1730 to Birmingham New Street.

City life, Jamaica Street. A Pendolino sneaks out of Central station bound for Euston.
(Author's collection)

In more recent years, planned diversions over the GSWR line via Barrhead – due to WCML engineering work – have tended to take place during weekends in the winter or spring. The last ever weekend to feature true loco-hauled diversions, before Pendolinos arrived on the WCML, was 20–21 March 2004 and this saw Virgin/EWS Class 47s and 57s dragging 87s and 90s dead-in-transit between Glasgow and Carlisle, as the GSWR is not electrified. This was also the last time a passenger train booked for 47 haulage would run in Scotland. In addition, WCML trains have occasionally been rerouted over the eastern side of the Cathcart Circle and via Bellshill and Holytown in recent years. Both these routes are electrified and therefore do not require a change to diesel traction.

As for the normal daytime service between Glasgow and Euston, the number of trains per day increased after electrification at the same time as schedules were accelerated. In early 1967, services from Glasgow were at 0740, 1015 (The Royal Scot), 1315 and 1615. By the early 1980s, departures were virtually every two hours, with passengers able to enjoy the comfort and space of Mark 3 coaches. The next major step, after the introduction of Pendolinos to the line, was an increase in frequency to make up the hourly Glasgow–Euston service – the fastest and most frequent yet. The December 2013 timetable change saw Virgin extend its Glasgow–Birmingham service to London Euston as well. Despite taking an hour longer, it offers cheaper fares than the main route, with an additional stop at Birmingham International to serve the airport.

By the 1990s, sleeper workings from Glasgow Central to London Euston had been reduced to just one train per night. Privatisation saw ScotRail take the operations over from InterCity and today the Glasgow train is known as the 'Lowland' portion of the Caledonian Sleeper, joining or combining at Carstairs with a separate portion to or from Edinburgh. The 'Highland' sleeper, which operates as a separate train, runs via Edinburgh to serve Fort William, Inverness and Aberdeen. There were also plans in the mid 1990s for 'Nightstar' international sleepers linking Glasgow with Paris, but this was eventually decided to be unviable.

The combined 'Lowland' sleeper is a long train, usually loading to sixteen coaches, with eight for Glasgow and eight for Edinburgh. Every day, after the early morning arrival of the 2350 from Euston at Glasgow Central, a light engine couples up at the other end to haul the empty coaching stock – complete with the Class 90 train locomotive – to Polmadie depot, before returning the whole formation to the station in the evening for the 2340 departure back to Euston. EWS/DB Schenker formerly used Class 47s on the ECS workings, but recent years have seen a variety of traction used, including 37s, 66s, 67s and 92s. It is not yet known if DB Schenker should continue to provide the motive power from April 2015, when all Scottish sleeper operations will be re-let to a new franchise separate from ScotRail. On the rolling stock side, refurbished interiors have been promised for the existing Mark 2 and 3 coaches.

Glasgow Central was also served for a very brief period by two Motorail services from Euston. A daytime train started in May 1993, joined by an overnight working a year later, but they were both prematurely withdrawn in 1995 with privatisation. BR had previously run Motorails from Stirling and Perth, serving destinations in the south such as Kensington Olympia and Sutton Coldfield.

Special trains

Charter trains now visit Glasgow more regularly than ever before, thanks to a growing railtour and preservation movement, which has seen heritage diesel locomotives become every bit as popular as their steam counterparts. Most specials have tended to originate south of the border, though the Scottish Railway Preservation Society (SRPS) has long been operating both steam- and diesel-hauled trains which traverse the city on their journey, often using stations there as their start or end points. Most of their diesel-hauled workings through the years have utilised Class 37s and 47s.

One exciting feature of charter trains – other than the motive power – is that they often head for the more obscure routes, including suburban lines which see virtually no traffic other than EMUs every day. Many through the years have used the low-level lines through Glasgow Queen Street and Central stations, the bulk being to or from the West Highland lines, as these provide an accessible route through the heart of the city that avoids reversal at the high-level termini. In recent years, more West Highland specials have started to use the North Clyde route via Yoker as an alternative to the more usual path via Singer. The Royal Scotsman luxury land-cruise train has been seen regularly since the 1980s from spring into autumn and its regular path to and from the Highlands sees it use the City Union line across the Clyde.

Joint ventures between the SRPS and Branch Line Society in recent years have taken in some rare track, such as the Milngavie branch, Cathcart Circle, Maryhill–Anniesland and Paisley Canal. Meanwhile, Pathfinder Railtours and Hertfordshire Railtours specialise in 'multi-traction' tours that have previously utilised freight locomotives such as classes 56, 60 and 66. As well as everyday working locomotives, preserved diesels such as Class 40 No. 40145 and 'Deltic' No. 55022 have also made appearances.

After their withdrawal in the 1960s, it would be a long time until a steam locomotive was able to work into Glasgow again. This was partly as a result of BR's policy banning steam from running under electric catenary without a diesel pilot. The ban was lifted in 1993, and on 18 September that year LNER

A2 Pacific No. 60532 *Blue Peter* was the first to run unassisted through the city, on its way up the GSWR main line from Carlisle towards Edinburgh. That same year saw specials from Glasgow Queen Street–Edinburgh with *Blue Peter* and A4 No. 60009 *Union of South Africa* to commemorate the 150th anniversary of the route via Polmont. There was also a special using LMS 'Black Five' No. 44871 *Sovereign* from Glasgow Central to East Kilbride and back (top-and-tailing with a Class 37) on 31 October 1993, to commemorate that route's 125th anniversary.

Steam has become an occasional feature in the city again since the 1990s, despite the difficulties in finding paths in the busy suburban timetable. Because of this, trains usually run at weekends, though there has been an increase in midweek running in recent times. Traditionally, the locomotives and stock used on the Fort William–Mallaig 'Jacobite' trains can be seen travelling on their way to and from Carnforth at the start and end of the summer season; usually routed via Coatbridge Central and Springburn. There has been little in the way of preserved steam at Queen Street, though Gresley K4 No. 61994 *The Great Marquess* has put in a couple of recent appearances.

Despite claims that there would be no steam allowed on the West Coast Main Line after introduction of a full Pendolino timetable, various locomotives have since travelled up to Glasgow Central, where the extended triangle of lines between Bridge Street, Shields and Larkfield junctions offers the chance to turn them after arrival. One particularly memorable tour was on 16–17 November 2006, when 'Princess Royal' class No. 6201 *Princess Elizabeth* ran between Preston and Glasgow to commemorate the 70th anniversary of her record-breaking run in 1936, which had seen the LMS Pacific make what was then the fastest ever non-stop journey time from London Euston. One wonders what her designer, Sir William Stanier, would have made of the modern Pendolinos!

9

Freight Traffic

Bulk flows

For a long time, the coal and steel industries were responsible for a large chunk of Scotland's rail freight business. Ravenscraig steelworks, near Motherwell, was one of the main railheads and its closure in 1992 left a huge hole in the country's network that it would not recover from until well after privatisation.

General Terminus harbour on the Clyde was still in heavy use throughout the 1970s, with iron ore transferred from cargo ships on to trains for onward transit to British Steel's Clyde Iron Works and Ravenscraig steel plant. Pairs of Class 20s provided the power for these workings, which were timed for 60mph running with a loaded train typically weighing in at 1,426 tonnes. This intensive series of workings, running day and night, served General Terminus until December 1979, when a new port at Hunterston took over as the railhead for the Ravenscraig ore traffic.

During the late 1980s, just before the run-down of Ravenscraig, there were around ten trains a day to and from Hunterston, with eight of these being iron ore and two coal. There were four terminals at Ravenscraig; No. 2 and No. 4 yards were for coal and iron ore respectively, and were adjacent to the Mossend–Wishaw via Holytown line. No.1 and No.3 yards were within British Steel's internal railway system, which used its own shunting locomotives and also served British Steel's nearby Clydesdale and Dalzell sites. The company's Gartcosh plant, which lay to the north of the city near Stepps, produced rolled steel destined for Lackenby via Mossend, until it shut in 1986.

Prior to Ravenscraig's closure, the iron ore and coal traffic was complemented by other incoming raw materials, such as limestone from Hardendale Quarry, Cumbria and Thrislington, County Durham, plus scrap metal from Dee Marsh. Finished steel coils went out electric-hauled (using pairs of 86s or 87s, thereafter single Class 90s) from Mossend Yard to Dee Marsh and Cardiff Tidal several times a day, after being conveyed on trip workings from Ravenscraig. The surviving Dalzell plant would later become part of the EWS/DB Schenker network

As well as carrying passenger services, the Maryhill line remains an important artery for freight to the West Highlands. On 6 January 2014, GBRf's 66735 heads the 6E45 0807 Fort William–North Blyth empty alumina train at Gilshochill, passing 156501 on the 1356 Glasgow Queen Street–Anniesland. (Author's collection)

and provide what is now the only remnant of this vastly reduced industry in Lanarkshire: the daily 6S58 Lackenby–Dalzell conveying incoming slabs and its empty return (6E30). Previously Dalzell could only be accessed via the private internal line with no direct main line connection, though a new spur was laid in the early 1990s for the new traffic.

Until the 1990s, Castle Cement's works at Gunnie, near Coatbridge, was served by a daily train from Clitheroe and this also utilised the hard-working Motherwell Class 37s double-headed. Today, there are regular workings from Clitheroe to Mossend for Castle Cement and Oxwellmains to Viewpark for Lafarge. They are operated by DB Schenker and Freightliner Heavy Haul respectively, though the latter was formerly EWS-worked. The Freightliner working is one of the few freights to use the Glasgow–Edinburgh via Shotts line regularly, along with GB Railfreight's Fort William–North Blyth bulk alumina train (6E45/6S45).

There are still regular coal trains travelling *through* the Glasgow area today, as a rise in traffic to destinations in Ayrshire and Fife has gradually taken over from the flows lost to the several loading and discharge sites that once stood in and around the city. During the 1970s, imported coal landed from ships at Rothesay Dock used to be loaded on to trains hauled by pairs of Class 20s, which then headed for Sighthill Yard before being sent to other destinations. The brief period

In appalling weather, DB Schenker's 66115 climbs through Carmyle, on the Whifflet line, with a loaded Hunterston–Longannet coal working on 30 December 2013. (Author's collection)

of traffic from the dock in the late 1980s would see both 20s and 26s on workings to and from Fife.

Merry-go-round workings of opencast coal became a big feature during the 1990s, with Ravenstruther terminal in Lanarkshire built in 1989, generating daily workings to Ayr Harbour (running via the WCML and Paisley) for onward transit by sea. Double-headed Railfreight coal sector Class 26s and 37s used to take charge of these before eventual replacement by 56s and 60s. Privatisation would then see EWS take over most coal traffic in Scotland and replace the usual 'HAA' hopper wagons with the larger 'HTAs'. The most regular workings seen in the Glasgow area today are those carrying imported product between Hunterston and Longannet power station, running to an intensive timetable and using the route Paisley–Shields Junction–Rutherglen–Coatbridge. There are also a number of trains which run to and from Mossend Yard.

Two of Glasgow's remaining coal-fired power stations in the 1970s – at Dalmarnock and Braehead – were converted to oil firing and these saw regular rail traffic from the petrochemicals complex at Grangemouth. A few years before Dalmarnock's closure in 1977 there were usually two loaded trains arriving per day on weekdays: an early morning 6V61 from Grangemouth behind two Class 37s and a lighter late-evening 6V62 working booked for a pair of 25s. Both returned

DRS Class 37s Nos 37218 and 37402 *Stephen Middlemore 23.12.1954–8.6.2013* take it easy on a short Hunterston–Sellafield nuclear-flask train at Cardonald, on 25 October 2013. (Author's collection)

empty during the morning. Braehead also received two trains a day, with pairs of 25s, 26s and 37s all seeing use. The power station here was located at the end of a branch line that left the main Glasgow–Paisley route at Cardonald, which would eventually be cut back to Deanside Transit depot.

Double-headed 25s also had booked oil turns between Grangemouth and the storage depots at Hawkhead (Paisley) and Bishopbriggs, though 20s and 37s would replace them before both sites shut in 1992 and 1993 respectively. Esso's depot at Bowling, near Dumbarton, received its oil by sea but used rail to transport it onwards to other destinations such as Kincardine power station in Fife. These days there are no remaining terminals in use in the Glasgow area, though Hawkhead still has its sidings in situ. Grangemouth still provides regular rail consignments to Dalston, Prestwick and Fort William for the time being, though these were almost lost in October 2013 when the plant on the Firth of Forth was a whisker away from being shut completely.

Distribution

Mossend Yard, near Motherwell, replaced Cadder and Sighthill marshalling yards in the early 1980s and soon became the overall hub of central Scotland's rail freight activities. A large part of this has been the distribution market; namely long-distance trains carrying a variety of general consumer goods across the border which are loaded or unloaded at Mossend to connect with road hauliers. It is these workings in particular that put up a good case for rail transport against road, as the alternative would be hundreds of thousands of extra lorries pounding up and down the motorways every year.

Part of the Down yard, at the western end of Mossend, is a railhead for logistics company PD Stirling, while the Up yard holds the Eurocentral terminal that was added in the early 1990s. The latter was constructed – complete with a car-loading facility – for predicted high volumes of Channel Tunnel traffic which never materialised, though it remains busy on the intermodal front nevertheless. Automotive trains were operated daily in recent years by EWS (cars and vans delivered to Scotland from Dagenham, Southampton and Portbury) and Freightliner (from Crewe) but are currently irregular.

Decades before, car-carrying trains also operated in the opposite fashion, delivering vehicles *from* Scotland. Leading British manufacturer Rootes (later Chrysler and Peugeot) formerly had a large factory in Linwood, near Paisley, which was a major assembly point for the Hillman Imp. It used rail to carry unfinished cars in kit form northbound and finished vehicles south, with sidings connecting to the Glasgow–Ayr main line adjacent to the Pressed Steel Company's works. Traffic was heavy for some time too, with up to three trains a day in each direction across the border during periods of peak demand, from Linwood to Gosford Green, Coventry, using single Class 25s or 47s, though a lack of demand or industrial strikes could see trains running empty.

Before the Linwood factory closed in 1981, its rail workings were altered several times, with other destinations being served as the company changed hands. The October 1975–May 1976 working timetable shows a 4M34 1110 Elderslie–Bell Green and 6V32 1740 Linwood–Morris Cowley, both running on Tuesdays only. There was also a Mondays-and-Thursdays-only train from Elderslie–Speke (Liverpool). The traction is of great interest: all of these were booked for Class 25 haulage over the as yet un-electrified line from Ayr as far as the Paisley Up goods loop, where a Class 81 or 85 electric would take over for the rest of the journey south.

Revolutionary BR Freightliner container flows started in the late 1950s, which resulted in the building of Gushetfaulds terminal near Polmadie. This was the main railhead for electric-hauled intermodal workings until the building of Coatbridge terminal in 1981, though it survived until the early 1990s when Mossend's Eurocentral was constructed.

The late 1990s would see a most welcome innovation started by EWS, when they began carrying containers for supermarket chain Safeway on overnight trains to Inverness and the north. Though only lasting for a few years, this paved the way for a much more successful partnership between Eddie Stobart and DRS delivering supplies for Tesco, which now produces several trains a day operating out of both Freightliner's Coatbridge facility and Mossend, towards Daventry in the south. These were joined by a daily train from Mossend to Inverness. What is most impressive is the sheer length of these workings, usually consisting of fourteen wagons each carrying two standard-size containers (effectively twenty-eight wagons). The amount of road congestion and consequent environmental effects avoided by these operations is therefore massive.

Elderslie, near Paisley, also joined the DRS intermodal network in late 2004, when W.H. Malcolm developed a loading facility on sidings alongside the Glasgow–Ayr main line to be served by a daily working from Grangemouth. With operations proving to be a success, the trains grew in length and have continued ever since, with Class 66s replacing the 37s initially used.

Wagonload

Traditional vacuum-braked mixed freight is another part of railway history that greatly diminished following Beeching and the end of steam, as much of it used branch lines which were lost as part of the cuts. As examined earlier, Glasgow had many such routes in and around the city, with some of these being freight-only latterly – Dawsholm, Ruchill and Lennoxtown to name but a few.

A 1980s view of Mossend Yard, near Motherwell, with Class 20 No. 20152 and an unidentified classmate on a short Speedlink working, while 20015 and an AC electric are visible to the right. By this period, it was more common to see 20s coupled nose-to-nose. (John Baker)

Cadder Yard, near Bishopbriggs, was the base for most mixed workings to the north. General merchandise in short-wheelbase vans and 16-ton open mineral wagons still accounted for much of the loads well into the 1970s before more block trains and air-braked wagons came in. Gravity-based 'hump shunting', performed by Class 08 pilots, was commonplace at Cadder, where there were twenty-two sidings in all within the Up and Down yards at either side of the Edinburgh–Glasgow main line.

There was always plenty of night-time activity at Cadder; weekday departures during the small hours included the 7A05 2315 to Aberdeen Craiginches (booked for either a Class 24 or 26), 8B03 0150 to Fort William and 8B05 0350 to Oban, which also ran on Saturdays. Type 2 motive power ruled at the yard throughout the 1970s, and as well as the more common 26s and 27s, 24s could appear on workings to Grangemouth and Dundee before they were withdrawn.

Another large hump yard, Sighthill Goods served destinations to the north, but also the south towards Carlisle and the West Coast Main Line, as it connected to the Springburn–Cumbernauld route, allowing movements along both sides of the Monklands triangle near Gartcosh. Its latter use was as a depot for National Carriers. High Street Goods – linked to what became the North Clyde line near Bellgrove – mainly served the south. Notable turns included daily workings out and back from either Sighthill or High Street to Carlisle, running day and night and employing Eastfield drivers on twelve-hour shifts. Class 27s and 37s were typical traction through the years. Other destinations served by these terminals included Leith South (Edinburgh), Aberdeen, Parkeston Quay and Bristol. Further east, Shettleston Yard became the base for many engineers trains, where another Class 08 would perform shunting duties.

The closure of High Street, Sighthill and Cadder yards by the early 1980s, to be replaced by Mossend, saw BR's wagonload freight service come under the Speedlink banner. By the latter half of that decade, Speedlink was responsible for the majority of freight traffic in Scotland, with internal Scottish workings being remarshalled at Mossend for onward transit in the longer trunk services, mainly across the border via the WCML. The same system of course saw loads from England and Wales brought to various customers' terminals in Scotland.

English-bound Speedlinks headed for locations such as Carlisle, Tyne Yard, Warrington, Bescot and Whitemoor. The Scottish internal workings were colourful and varied, using motley collections of air-braked wagons and locomotives from various Railfreight (and non-Railfreight) pools. Within the city itself, Deanside Transit distribution depot near Cardonald was served on the line towards the erstwhile Braehead power station with a variety of cargo – often food and drink – usually handled in sliding wall vans. Further west, there were workings to Bishopton and Greenock, serving a Royal Ordnance Factory producing explosives and a sugar works respectively. The Dalry Roche ICI plant saw coal and chemicals transported, while trains to Lugton carried fertiliser. MoD traffic also worked beyond Lugton on the Giffen branch line.

Daily traffic to the West Highlands had varied loads and offered guaranteed Class 37 haulage from the mid 1980s onwards. Oil tankers were carried regularly to Oban, while Mossend–Fort William workings usually conveyed oil and china clay northbound, plus timber, paper and aluminium slabs in the opposite direction. Mossend–Inverness workings conveyed oil, timber and grain, though Inverness was also served each day by Millerhill Yard in Edinburgh. Aberdeen was the other main destination in the north and workings to and from Mossend conveyed all kinds of materials, including starch, fertiliser, cement, chemicals and oil.

With so many short-to-medium-length trains, which often conveyed just one or two wagons for each individual customer, Speedlink was never going to be the most cost-effective method of transport. The sector was disbanded in July 1991 as a recession gripped the country, with many wagonload services being withdrawn (either then or over the next few years) or combined to make longer trains. Railfreight Distribution's operating loss was reduced by nearly £34 million thanks to these measures. After that, most freight workings from Mossend would be concentrated on just a few selected major railheads around the country, such as Fort William, Inverness and Aberdeen.

EWS would revive the wagonload network following privatisation with their 'Enterprise' operations, though it would take a few years for traffic to really pick up, before shrinking once again. J.G. Russell at Deanside was one of their prime customers, being one of the few long-distance railheads served when this network was first established. Its incoming traffic included one of the heaviest workings in the country, which conveyed pet food in VGA vans from Wisbech in Cambridgeshire, though this ceased to run after the millenium. Deanside was thereafter served by a daily Enterprise from Mossend only, but there is no traffic at the time of writing.

EWS also soon established a new Enterprise with vans and containers running from Grangemouth docks to Mossend, which is thriving to this day. Timber haulage from the Highlands expanded into several different daily flows which combined to form the daily Enterprise from Mossend to Warrington Arpley, but this market has since gone over to road and sea haulage completely, leaving no more Enterprises to the north save for Aberdeen and Grangemouth, as block trains tend now to suffice for the remaining traffic. There are no longer any private company freight terminals within the city receiving traffic, though it is possible new ventures could be started eventually, despite the sluggish economy.

The vast reduction in wagonload traffic has also meant less need for a shunter at Mossend; previously there were two EWS/DB Schenker Class 08s in all-day use on weekdays but recent years have seen it reduced to just one. Shunting is performed where possible by the train engines, with DB locomotives stabling in the Down sidings and Freightliner in the Up when not in use, adjacent to both companies' respective train crew depots. This includes Freightliner 86s and 90s that have worked into Coatbridge terminal. There are proposals to expand Mossend further in the coming years which, if they go ahead, will see an 'International Railfreight Park' established by PD Stirling, with longer trains running to new destinations all over the Continent to complement Eurocentral.

Certain through-workings pausing at Mossend change from electric to diesel traction or vice versa, particularly trains bound for Ayrshire. A project undertaken in the winter of 2007–08 saw the electrification of the 'Burma Road' spur at Shields Junction which dives under the main line and gives trains from the Paisley direction access to Polmadie and Mossend (via the 'Clydesdale' linking line), and this was supposed to have paved the way for electric haulage the whole way, such as Class 92s on coal trains. But as yet, this has still to happen and Class 66s remain.

Mail and parcels

Until the opening of Shieldmuir Royal Mail terminal in February 1998, a nightly (excluding Saturdays) travelling post office (TPO) train ran each way between Glasgow Central and London Euston. It was known in steam days as the 'West Coast Postal', with a portion to Aberdeen joining or separating at Carstairs. The Up working was the train involved in the 1963 Great Train Robbery. After Beeching, they became known simply as the 'Up Special' and 'Down Special' mail trains, with the headcodes 1M44 and 1S09 respectively.

Class 40s, then Class 50s handled the nightly TPO until electrification of the WCML saw 86s and 90s used, before operations then passed over to Rail Express Systems. This saw a move to Class 325 EMUs and the train's route cut back from Glasgow to Birmingham, before being extended in October 1995 to run from Glasgow to Cardiff. The transfer of operations to Shieldmuir saw this continue, along with several daytime postal workings, until Royal Mail quit using rail traffic in 2003. It was revived shortly after by GBRf.

While letters were dealt with on the TPO, parcels and newspaper traffic was handled in separate trains, principally running from either Central station or the goods yard on Salkeld Street, which became known as Glasgow Parcels Station. One of the best-known workings was the heavy Glasgow–Manchester Red Bank sidings empty newspaper train, which could load up to twenty vans. Most other parcels was carried during the hours of darkness, with several different workings a night, to destinations including London Euston, Crewe, Bristol and Carlisle, though traffic declined considerably into the 1990s. A couple of decades previously, there were still some shorter-distance trains to Kilmarnock and Carlisle, mostly using Class 25s or 37s.

It must also be remembered that well into the 1980s many loco-hauled inter-regional passenger trains running out of Central and Queen Street would also convey a parcels van, or at the very least had plenty of room available in the guard's compartment of the brake coach for large amounts of luggage, parcels, bicycles and other items. The introduction of Sprinter units saw such luxuries disappear.

10

Depot Profiles

Eastfield (65A/ED)

Eastfield traction depot, near Cowlairs, has long provided the motive power for trains out of Queen Street station on lines to the north of the city, to as far afield as Inverness and Aberdeen. This tradition goes right back to 1904 when the original steam shed was opened by the North British Railway, before it passed over to the LNER and then BR. Eastfield's perfect location and large size saw it kept in use by BR at the end of steam and converted into a diesel shed while most others in Glasgow were shut. It would then go on to be known as Eastfield TMD.

BR blue is the only colour to be seen at Eastfield shed on 16 October 1982, with a line-up of classes 08, 20, 26 and 27. A few years later, Type 2s would be largely replaced by Class 37s and 47s. (Jules Hathaway)

The depot would receive the usual refinements to make it suitable for diesels, including a modern main shed building to replace the original stone structure, with a small part of it reserved for the resident DMU fleet. There were eleven shed roads with additional outside siding space, where most of the serviceable locomotive fleet was usually stabled. In addition, there were the facilities to perform all but the heaviest maintenance on locomotives (overhauls were concentrated on St Rollox works) and the later closure of other engine depots such as Polmadie would see more repairs carried out there as a result. Other features around the yard included an undercover fuelling point, wheel lathe (used for re-profiling wheelsets) and staff training rooms.

At its height, Eastfield had an allocation of around 160 main line diesels (through the years mainly classes 08, 20, 24, 25, 26, 27, 37, 47), 20 shunters and 40 DMUs, but was dogged by a lack of space to accommodate them (though DMUs would also stable at Cowlairs carriage sidings). In the 1980s, the depot was one of the first on BR to start personalising its locomotives, particularly with the famous 'Scottie Dog' motif and various unusual liveries adopted on their 37s and 47s. However, the locomotive allocation started to dwindle with the end of loco-hauled passenger trains and closure in 1992 saw the entire site eventually cleared except for a couple of sidings. To mark its closure, resident Class 26s Nos 26001/007 were repainted into original BR green livery in the summer of 1992 and hauled various special charters for ScotRail over the next year. No. 26001 had received the name *Eastfield* at its home depot on 26 July 1991.

Luckily the site of the old TMD was not built over and this allowed ScotRail's new 2004 depot to be laid easily in the same place. Now home to classes 156, 158 and 170, today's Eastfield depot is smaller in size and allows for stabling and light maintenance only.

Polmadie (66A/PO)

Polmadie depot, near Rutherglen, has a long and proud history of being a top link shed, used for servicing locomotives working up the WCML into Glasgow Central. It has been in existence for nearly 140 years, after being built by the Caledonian Railway in 1875, subsequently taken over by the LMS and eventually converted for diesel use. 'Duchess' and 'Princess Royal' Pacifics were soon replaced by classes 40, 47 and 50, alongside 20s, 27s and 37s used for local freight duties.

After full electrification of the WCML, it was decided to close Polmadie as an engine shed, but it would continue in use as a carriage depot, being operated today by Alstom and used to service the Virgin Pendolino and Voyager fleets. Cleaning and maintenance of both the Glasgow- and Edinburgh-bound Caledonian Sleepers takes place here during the day. The depot celebrated its

By July 1968, the old steam shed at Polmadie was still in place but taken over by diesels. From left to right are two Class 47s, three Class 20s (including two inside the shed), three Class 08s, a Class 17 and two more 47s. A breakdown crane also sticks out to the left of the building. (Allan Trotter, Eastbank Model Railway Club)

125th birthday on 16 September 2000 with an open day, which saw the naming of Virgin locomotives 47851 *Strathclyde* (formerly carried by 47706) and 87023 *Polmadie*.

Motherwell (66B/ML)

Another ex-Caledonian depot, established in 1866, Motherwell was traditionally always more of a home for freight locomotives; most notably those working to the local steel plants such as Ravenscraig and also Mossend Yard. It is situated alongside Braidhurst goods loops next to the junction of the WCML and Coatbridge lines north of Motherwell station, and its original brick-built eight-road shed still stands to this day. After the end of steam, it became home to a large diesel allocation, mostly classes 20, 26 and 37, but never hosted electrics except latterly Class 325s, as the wires on the main line never extended in there.

Class 37/0 and 37/3 variants used on the steel and coal traffic were probably the locomotives most identified with Motherwell Traction Maintenance Depot, for their large-font numbers and depiction of the shed mascot – the 'Leaping Salmon' – on their bodysides. Several were also named after the industrial landmarks they served, such as *Clydesdale, Dalzell* and *Glengarnock*, while the 'Leaping Salmon' was replaced in the 1990s by a 'Hammer and Anvil' logo as the diesel allocation was boosted with the closure of Eastfield TMD.

TransRail, then EWS, would take over the depot after BR, with classes 56, 60, 66 and 67 soon becoming a familiar sight in the yard. EWS days saw as many as thirty-two 66s officially allocated to the depot at one point but this was a paper exercise more than anything else. This included 66095–114; the twenty locomotives initially fitted with RETB equipment for working the West Highland and Inverness–Wick/Thurso lines.

A major fire in August 2001, caused by a faulty gas-powered steam generator, saw most of the shed roof destroyed, with only some of it being rebuilt as the site was run down over the next few years. Condemned locomotives soon started to outnumber the serviceable motive power at the TMD before it closed completely in 2007, leaving Strathclyde without any traditional locomotive depot to its name. It was deemed sufficient to replace Motherwell with a rather spartan locomotive stabling and fuelling point at Mossend. However, the depot has been brought back into administrative use for Network Rail and as a wagon repair facility for DRS.

Corkerhill (67A/CK)

Corkerhill depot, situated near the station of the same name, was the Glasgow and South Western Railway's main shed in Scotland and played host to express locomotives which worked into Glasgow St Enoch station from the south, amongst others. After the end of steam, it was kept open for maintaining much of the DMU fleet working into Glasgow Central and overhead wires would later be added in 1986 when the line from Shields Junction was electrified. This enabled classes 303, 314 and 318 to be stabled and receive light repairs there too.

The main class to be seen at Corkerhill today is Class 156, with all members of the ScotRail fleet now based there. ScotRail is currently trialling a new environmentally friendly system to clean the units using thousands of litres of rainwater collected in the shed roof, something which could potentially be adopted at other depots.

Shields Road (GW)

ScotRail's Shields depot, colloquially known as Shields Road, is a purpose-built EMU depot, having been opened by BR in May 1967 when the lines to Gourock and Wemyss Bay were electrified. Its location close to Central station meant that it was used for maintaining all Class 303 and 311 units used on the lines to Cathcart, Neilston and Newton in addition to the Clyde coast. Locomotives were also seen there until the early 1990s. In addition to the Class 81s based at Shields, others such as 87s and 90s used to visit for minor maintenance, including 'A' and 'B' exams.

C4 overhauls, which involve bogie changes, are undertaken on units at Shields, with anything more extensive having to be done at Springburn works or Brodie's in Kilmarnock. Coaching stock also used to receive attention here, including use of the wheel lathe shop, which is also used occasionally today by visiting locomotives and DMUs. The depot now has twelve running roads, with four of these running into the main shed building and three serving a newer shed which was added recently for the servicing of Class 380s. All ScotRail EMU classes can now be seen frequently in the yard.

Yoker (YO)

Yoker TMD opened in June 1987 to service EMUs on the North Clyde line, replacing the maintenance facilities at Hyndland and Bridgeton Central which closed at the same time. It is situated alongside the main line and what was formerly the junction for the Rothesay Dock branch line near Clydebank and is used for the cleaning and stabling of units only. The layout consists mainly of a set of sidings on either side of the depot – ten at the west end and twelve at the east – with an automatic washing plant at each end too. Classes 318, 320 and 334 are all commonplace here.

The modern installations at Yoker, with ScotRail unit Nos 320320, 318261 and 318270 all stabled next to the maintenance platforms at the east end of the yard on Sunday 5 January 2014. (Author's collection)

Preserved LNER K4 No. 61994 *The Great Marquess* passes the site of Waterside Junction, near Lenzie, on the Thornton–Fort William leg of the 'Great Britain VI' steam tour, on 25 April 2013. The Gresley 2-6-0 spent much of her working life based only a few miles away at Eastfield depot. (Author's collection)

LMS 'Duchess' Pacifics used to have regular passenger turns working between Crewe and Perth. On 6 September 2013, No. 46233 *Duchess of Sutherland* retraces this route past Greenfoot level crossing, near Glenboig, with the '75th Anniversary Special' from Sheffield. At this time, the Cumbernauld line was undergoing electrification work and, weeks later, views like this would be ruined by overhead wire masts. (Author's collection)

A general view of BRML Springburn works and MC Metals scrapyard as viewed from the nearby high flats in October 1991. The scrapyard shunter 20148 collects coaches for cutting, while four withdrawn 'Peak' diesels can just be made out languishing in the sidings. The main workshops can be seen to the right. (Jules Hathaway)

By 1990, Sprinter units were in abundance at Glasgow Queen Street. On 23 June, Provincial-liveried 156466 departs under the Cathedral Street bridge, while a Strathclyde PTE example waits at platform 1. (David Webster)

Saturday afternoon crowds on the Queen Street station concourse. (Author's collection)

The 2350 Glasgow–Euston 'Lowland' sleeper awaits departure from Central station's platform 10, behind DB Schenker red-liveried Class 90 No. 90018. 17 January 2014. (Author's collection)

A view of Glasgow Central's complex series of approach lines across the Clyde, with Class 314 No. 314202 arriving on the 1400 service from Neilston and Class 156 Sprinter No. 156439 on the 1355 from East Kilbride, 28 November 2013. (Author's collection)

Train and boat meet on a gloomy day down by the Broomielaw. A pair of ScotRail Class 156s cross the bridge into Central station, as a training lifeboat from the nearby nautical college passes underneath on the Clyde, 7 March 2012. (Author's collection)

Class 303 and 311 EMUs were almost identical from the outside. This April 1978 view at Glasgow Central shows 303034 on the left, alongside 311101. Both carry plain BR 'corporate blue' livery. (Tom Noble)

A wonderful scene at Gushetfaulds Freightliner terminal, near Polmadie, in June 1968, showing several BR lorries alongside the container loading cranes. A Brush Type 4 (Class 47) can be seen in the yard. (Allan Trotter, Eastbank Model Railway Club)

A Virgin Pendolino snakes its way through Rutherglen, nearing its journey's end on the 0730 Euston–Glasgow on 21 August 2013. The disused main line platforms of Rutherglen station are out of site to the left, while the footbridge in the background is used for passenger access to the present platforms on the Argyle line. (Author's collection)

The environment of Maxwell Park station on the Cathcart Circle contrasts strongly with the concrete jungle of nearby Glasgow city centre. On the pleasant evening of 8 August 2013, 314213 leaves with the 1745 Glasgow Central–Newton. Both the train and the immaculate station are painted in the erstwhile SPT carmine and cream colours. (Author's collection)

The autumn sun sets over Busby Junction on the Glasgow–Kilmarnock main line, as Sprinter 156508 takes the East Kilbride branch on 19 November 2013. (Author's collection)

Floral displays at Burnside, one of many ScotRail stations in the city to be adopted by volunteers. (Author's collection)

Class 318 No. 318255 calls at the tight underground confines of Argyle Street station on 11 January 2014, with the 1106 Larkhall–Dalmuir. (Author's collection)

Before the coming of the Class 50s, English Electric Class 40s worked regularly into Glasgow on the West Coast Main Line. D264 is captured at Newton in January 1968, unusually at the head of a coal train. (Allan Trotter, Eastbank Model Railway Club)

A short eastbound train of Esso oil tankers makes its way through Dalmuir Park behind an unidentified English Electric Type 1 (Class 20) in August 1968. Not long after, this station was renamed simply 'Dalmuir', following the closure of nearby Dalmuir Riverside. (Allan Trotter, Eastbank Model Railway Club)

Class 318 No. 318259 arrives at the winter wonderland of Scotstounhill, with the 1149 Springburn–Dalmuir service on 13 February 2013. (Author's collection)

It's amazing what you can find in your local supermarket car park! 'Deltic' No. 55022 *Royal Scots Grey* – on hire to GB Railfreight – passes the site of Partickhill goods yard, hauling an empty Class 334 unit from Yoker to Kilmarnock for refurbishment on 17 June 2013. The two tanker wagons are provided to give the train adequate brake force, while the third vehicle is a translator coach which allows locomotives to couple to modern EMUs. (Author's collection)

The modernised Subway station at Hillhead, with car No. 107 leading an outer circle train. Note the new SPT orange and silver colour scheme, plus the additional platform used for the inner circle. (Author's collection)

SPT carmine and cream was the dominant colour scheme to be found on Glasgow's railways for several years after privatisation. On 12 June 2008, Class 170 Turbostar No. 170478 arrives at Springburn with the 0944 Falkirk Grahamston–Glasgow Queen Street, while a Class 320 waits in the electrified bay platform with a Dalmuir service. Both units will head towards Glasgow city centre despite facing in opposite directions, as the former uses the Cowlairs chord line to take virtually a 180-degree turn towards Queen Street high-level. (Author's collection)

Glasgow Works, Springburn (ZH)

Following its acquisition by BREL, the ex-Caledonian Railway St Rollox workshops became responsible for heavy overhauls and major repairs to locomotives, multiple units and rolling stock used all over the country but particularly those based in Scotland. A familiar trademark which had long been a feature of the works, continuing into the 1980s, was the application of larger-than-normal bodyside numerals on locomotives outshopped there.

Ironically, the place which once built locomotives would soon be responsible for scrapping them. To start with, as locomotive withdrawals started to mount in the late 1970s, the Springburn compound was used to store condemned machines, using yard space which became available as the facility's overhaul workload started to shrink. Then in 1987, part of the site was acquired by MC Metals Processing Ltd, who developed it into one of the largest locomotive scrapyards in Britain. It was the only facility in the country able to carry out asbestos removal and as a result, many Class 31s, 33s and 45s met their end here, alongside other types.

In 1988, BREL passed over to the private sector and the works at St Rollox became British Rail Maintenance Ltd (BRML) Springburn. Late in the 1990s,

A sad scene at the MC Metals yard on 19 October 1991, with several once-proud diesels reduced to nothing more than their cabs. Nos 31260, 45052 (unofficially named *Nimrod*) and three Class 20s are the locomotives, alongside the remains of another Class 31, No. 31226. (Jules Hathaway)

MC Metals shut down as most of the former BR land was redeveloped and became unrecognisable, with Tesco and Costco superstores, plus a large Royal Mail sorting office built over it. The remaining railway works was scaled down to a small fan of sidings serving the main workshops, operated jointly by Babcock and Siemens until Alstom took over in 2002. It changed hands again in 2007, being acquired by Railcare Ltd.

It is pleasing to report that despite major cutbacks through the decades, Springburn works still has a heavy output to this day under German company Knorr-Bremse Rail Systems (UK). Recent years have seen DRS and other English-based operators such as Northern Rail send their locomotives and DMUs here for refurbishment, though ScotRail is its biggest customer at present, with Springburn responsible for much of the recent Saltire re-livery programme. Full overhauls have also been given to classes 314, 318 and 320.

The plant survived a major scare in July 2013 when Railcare went into administration and thirty-three jobs were cut, in addition to another 118 at the firm's Wolverton works near Milton Keynes. Just as the future was looking very bleak, Knorr-Bremse took over and the Glasgow works lived to fight another day, preserving over 170 years of railway history in the area. It has been business as usual at Springburn ever since.

11

Signalling and Infrastructure

Signalling

The era since Beeching has seen major resignalling projects take place over the vast majority of Britain's rail network. Chiefly, this has involved the programme of replacing traditional, mechanical signal boxes and the semaphore signals they control. This process was far more rapid in large cities such as Glasgow, where large signalling centres or power boxes are ideal for controlling busy sections of line with complex trackwork. The first piece of the jigsaw was for more simplified train movements in and out of the two large termini, Central and Queen Street, duly completed by 1967, by which time both had their colour lights and nearby power boxes (at Bridge Street and Cowlairs) fully commissioned.

Two BR green Class 25s scuttle past Polmadie signal box next to the depot in June 1968. (Allan Trotter, Eastbank Model Railway Club)

Upgrades to the WCML associated with electrification involved all mechanical boxes along the Scottish section being closed between 1971 and 1974. The route would instead come under the control of Glasgow Central Signalling Centre (Central–Rutherglen East Junction) and the new Motherwell Signalling Centre (Cambuslang–Kirkpatrick). The former gradually had its area of control extended; in early 1973 it replaced the boxes at Larkfield Junction, Polmadie, Shawfield, Rutherglen station, Rutherglen Junction and Cambuslang goods. From 1973 to 1974 it also gradually assumed control towards Busby Junction and the East Kilbride branch. Its successor – the West of Scotland Signalling Centre (WSSC) at Cowlairs – took over the whole aforementioned area in December 2008, and over the course of the next two decades it will have its jurisdiction widened even further, taking over from Motherwell SC amongst others.

With the north- and south-side electrification programmes during the 1960s, there was large-scale removal of semaphore signals, though various mechanical boxes were kept in place and converted to control colour lights instead. A number of these were on the North Clyde line and remained in use until the 1989–91 Yoker resignalling scheme. Summer 1989 saw the boxes at Clydebank Dock Junction, Singer and Dalmuir Park all close, followed in the autumn by Hyndland and High Street Junction, with all of these areas now overseen by the new Yoker Integrated Electronic Control Centre (IECC). Completion of the £20 million programme between 1990 and 1991 saw the boxes at Milngavie, Westerton, Bellgrove, Parkhead North, Shettleston, Heatheryknowe, Coatbridge Sunnyside Junction and Airdrie also accept their last trains.

Pockets of semaphores survived in the north-east outskirts of Glasgow until the Cowlairs resignalling scheme in early 1999, when the remaining boxes at Cadder, Sighthill Junction, Gartcosh, Gartsherrie, Garnqueen North, Greenfoot and Cumbernauld were shut and demolished. The 1956-built box at Cowlairs was replaced by a more modern successor.

To the south of the city, 1960s electrification had brought new power boxes at Muirhouse Junction and Cathcart. The former only lasted until September 1973, while the latter survived until April 2013, when the Cathcart Circle and Neilston lines became yet another section under the control of the growing Cowlairs WSSC.

Station features

The Beeching cuts sparked some serious cost-cutting by BR all over the country, whereby the majority of intermediate stations which remained open would be modernised and stripped down to become simple, no-frills affairs, redesigned for the sake of being practical more than anything else. This was particularly true for suburban networks like Strathclyde and a look at most stations today will reveal that a large number of them are unstaffed, with most original buildings disused or demolished and replaced by 'bus shelter' waiting rooms; but at the same time, most now benefit from the very best twenty-first-century technology and passenger access facilities that are second to none. CCTV, public address systems, LED information boards and long platforms (with tactile warning strips for the blind or visually impaired) are some of the most obvious improvements made by ScotRail in recent years.

There are some stations which survived BR's rationalisation relatively unscathed and retain their traditional architecture to this day. Maxwell Park on the Cathcart Circle is one of the most iconic, having had its original walk-through, two-tier main building fully refurbished and repainted in 2000, complete with heritage Victorian platform lamps. The Cathcart District Railway had a distinctive style in general which is evident today all around the Circle, all stations having island platforms, either in tenement-shrouded cuttings or placed above street level with access via a subway. The connecting Cathcart–Neilston and Newton routes are similar in this respect. In addition, several stops on this group of lines still retain their chalet-like main buildings and are still staffed on a part-time basis.

Pollokshaws West: Glasgow's oldest station. As well as the restored main building, train-shaped flower baskets on the platforms add character. (Author's collection)

Pollokshaws West, on the line to Barrhead and Kilmarnock, was opened by the Glasgow, Barrhead and Neilston Direct Railway in 1848, making it the oldest surviving station in the city. Its large B-listed main building was fully restored in 2013 by the Glasgow Building Preservation Trust and is now in use as a cycle resource centre, being one of the success stories of ScotRail's 'Adopt a Station' initiative. This has seen local volunteers breathe new life into some very tired-looking suburban stations, by tidying the platforms and giving them some character with the addition of features such as flowers. As a result, the city's railway environment now looks arguably more presentable than ever before.

Rail passengers in Glasgow can now feel safer than ever, as all stations in the city are now fitted with CCTV, controlled from a special Customer Service Centre housed in Paisley Gilmour Street station. The past decade has seen a major increase in the provision of cameras, which is especially important given that many stations are unstaffed, for certain times of the day at least. In addition, all ScotRail multiple units except for the Class 314s now carry onboard CCTV.

Locations to get the 'Adopt a Station' treatment include Bearsden, Cardonald, Carntyne, Duke Street, Easterhouse, Shawlands and Westerton, but there are many more. Milngavie was famous for its beautiful presentation long before the days of ScotRail, having been the winner of many awards through the decades for its immaculate buildings and floral displays. The small terminus reached its 150th anniversary in 2013 and the main stone building (in existence since the station opening in 1863) remains fully functional and open with a ticket office and waiting area, plus a substantial platform awning still standing in as-built condition.

Certain stations along the North Clyde and Argyle lines utilise island platforms, such as Garscadden, Anderston and Bellgrove. The 1960-built Hyndland – also an island – was unusually constructed with a footbridge linking it to the residential area on its west side (Churchill Drive) but an underpass to the east side (with a pathway to Gartnavel Hospital), until it got its new footbridge in 2012, which provides access to either side.

Newton is an especially interesting location, as its two platform faces only serve the slow lines while the fast lines of the WCML bypass it. Prior to electrification of the line to Kirkhill and Cathcart, there had also been platforms serving the fast lines. There is now a double-lead junction at each end to serve the routes to Kirkhill and Hamilton respectively, west and east crossovers to the WCML and a turnback siding at the east end for the Glasgow–Newton terminating service.

Newton received further track layout enhancements in late 2013, when an extra connecting line was laid between the platforms and the WCML at the west end, allowing more flexibility than the single-lead junction originally in use. A double-lead towards Kirkhill had of course been installed shortly after the 1991 accident there. A 245-space car park was added to the station in recent years, as was a footbridge with lifts similar to that at Dalmuir and Hyndland; passengers previously had to use the subway beneath the platforms.

Electrification

The electrified lines in Glasgow are all powered by the standard 25kV AC system, though certain sections which had limited clearance due to overbridges, tunnels or cuttings used 6.25kV in the early days. The whole of the Cathcart Circle initially came into this category, but half of it became 25kV in 1974. Class 303s had dual-voltage capability to enable use of both types. However, the latter part of the 1970s would see the whole Strathclyde network become 25kV, after the trackbed was lowered in the required locations.

The now electrified Paisley Canal terminus, built on the site of the old through-station closed in 1983. The old track formation and retaining walls can be clearly seen. (Author's collection)

The Paisley Canal line is slightly different to others in the electrified network. ScotRail and Network Rail were winners at the 2013 National Transport Awards in the 'Partnership of the Year' category, for their work on putting the branch 'under the wires' in 2012. They gained this recognition after working together to complete the project at a cost of £12 million, less than half of the £28 million budget originally put forward. This 'economy electrification' was achieved after ScotRail waived their right to disruption compensation and after authorisation was given for a lower-than-normal wire height beneath certain overbridges as well as a 70ft-long 'neutral' section, which meant less cost on clearance work. The forthcoming electrification of the Whifflet line is expected to utilise similar techniques.

12

The Glasgow Subway

The Underground, the 'Tube', the 'Clockwork Orange', call it what you will; the Glasgow Subway has been a cornerstone of life in the city for nearly 120 years. It was opened on 14 December 1896 by the Glasgow District Subway Company to provide a new means of transport between the residential and industrial areas in the west end and the city centre, at a time when congestion on the streets was a becoming a problem. It was initially the only underground railway in the world to use cable haulage for traction, before being converted to electric power, and is now the only wholly-underground line network in the UK outside London.

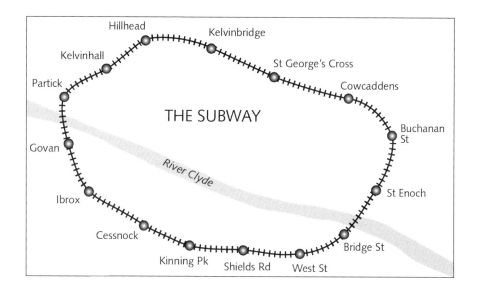

The early system

The line itself is a 6½-mile-long loop built to a unique gauge of 4ft (1,220mm), consisting of an 'inner circle' and 'outer circle' tunnelled throughout between stations. During building from 1891 to 1896, all fifteen stations were provided with island platforms, while the 11ft (3.35m)-diameter tunnels were reinforced with bricks and mortar for the most part, the remainder utilising cast iron. The two cables that pulled the trains were steam powered and ran at a constant speed of 13mph, controlled from a building in Scotland Street near Kinning Park, while trains moved or stopped by simply gripping or releasing the cables. In 1923 the Glasgow Corporation Tramways Department took over operations from Glasgow District Subway Co.

In 1935 the Underground was converted from cable to third-rail electric power, with the initial journey time of forty minutes for a full-circle run reduced to twenty-eight minutes. The original wooden-bodied two-car trainsets would continue in use after conversion to electric traction, these being made up of one motor and one trailer coach, with a cab at one end only and doors on just one side. Transferring them between the running lines and maintenance depot at Govan was a complex affair, requiring the use of a crane to lift them to and from the track.

A quiet platform at St George's Cross less than two years before the Underground closed for modernisation, as an inner circle train calls on 4 December 1975. Note the original wooden-bodied stock, as well as the station master's cabin at the platform end. (Tom Noble)

Modernisation

The same electric system with the same trains continued in use on the Subway over the next few decades, but by the early 1970s it was in decline, with passenger numbers down to 10 million a year after a previous high of over 35 million in 1949–50 (not helped by a decreasing population). Fresh from Beeching and the main railway cutbacks, the Underground would have to be modernised to survive. Glasgow Corporation conducted a review of the system in the early 1970s and concluded that a lengthy closure would be necessary to allow a complete refurbishment of every aspect of the railway from top to bottom. A lack of investment following the Second World War had been cited for the downturn in patronage and increasing unreliability of the services, and this could not go on. The Corporation would be taken over in June 1973 by Greater Glasgow PTE, which would carry the proposals forward.

One improvement identified was the need to integrate the Subway more with other modes of transport, particularly road. By now, it was found that around 70 per cent of passengers using the tube were using the bus or car too on their daily journeys, so park-and-ride facilities were suggested for Kelvinbridge, Partick and Shields Road as one way forward. This also saw the new Partick main line railway/underground interchange station planned next to the bus station, thereby closing the existing Merkland Street tube station which sat only yards away in the same area. But apart from Patrick, there were to be no changes to station siting, no station closures and no extension or deviation from the existing trackbed, other than a new depot siding at Govan.

The Underground ended up closing earlier than originally planned for refurbishment, as cracks were discovered in the roof of Govan Cross station in 1977. There was an initial temporary closure period from 24 March to 2 May that year, but it ended up shutting again on the 21 May when the same problem resurfaced, seven days before the scheduled closure date in advance of the upgrade work. Keeping the line open any longer would have run the risk of something more catastrophic taking place, so it went ahead there and then. At this time, the service had a basic three-minute frequency Monday–Saturday from 6 a.m. to 11 p.m., and every four minutes on a Sunday.

Extensive rebuilding work saw the ground opened up above stations, while one running line remained open to allow the use of track maintenance vehicles for transporting construction materials. The stations were all given massive facelifts, with light-coloured platform and wall tiles creating a much brighter atmosphere. The opportunity was also taken to rename four of them. Merkland Street was replaced by the new interchange named simply 'Partick', Govan Cross became just Govan, Copland Road became Ibrox and Partick Cross became Kelvinhall.

Furthermore, escalators were provided for platform access at nine stations: Partick, Govan, Shields Road, St Enoch, Buchanan Street, Cowcaddens, St George's Cross, Kelvinbridge and Hillhead. The other stations remained steps-only due to being closer to ground level. Additional side platforms were added to boost capacity at Hillhead, Ibrox and Buchanan Street, while Partick, Govan and St Enoch got all-new platforms at either side to replace the traditional island layout. In addition, new automatic ticket gates were installed at all stops on the line.

The new trains built for the modernised Underground marked a massive technological advancement. Automatic control was launched, with a 'driver' in the cab of each unit essentially to supervise more than anything, to ensure the automatic equipment was working properly at all times. This included checking that the train was braking effectively, stopping at stations in the correct position and being there to open and close the electronic doors. After being activated by the driver at each stop, the trains would run automatically from station to station, with trackside beacons electronically transmitting instructions, effectively following a predetermined course that adjusted itself to speed changes along the way. A manual driving mode would also be available, specifically for each train to access the modernised Broomloan depot in Govan. A new spur was laid to give the shed a direct track connection up a steep incline instead of having to use a hoist, with a crossover allowing movements from both the inner and outer circles.

The new trains themselves were of all-steel construction, built by Metro-Cammell in 1977–78 for operation as two-car units. Each formation was made up out of thirty-three power cars (numbered 101–33), all identical to each another with a driving cab at one end and a maximum speed of 54km/h. They were outshopped in a striking new orange livery which would soon be rolled out on the standard-gauge railway and this meant that – unlike on BR lines – Underground staff had to wear yellow high-visibility vests (not orange) to stand out.

Her Majesty the Queen opened the new Glasgow Underground (as it had been officially titled since 1937) at a ceremony staged at Buchanan Street station on 1 November 1979, but teething problems delayed the official opening for several months, with public services finally starting on 16 April 1980. A full circuit of the line was now cut down to a best time of twenty-four minutes, with a four-minute frequency at peak times, reduced to between six and eight minutes off-peak. There were no Sunday trains but there was at least the lengthening of some rush-hour trains to three-car formations for the first time, which meant in turn that some platforms had to be extended for them to fit.

The public were impressed by the rebuilt Underground, which proved to be cleaner, faster and more reliable than in pre-1977 days. Passenger levels increased, but this was very gradual to begin with, as the city recovered from economic hardship into the 1980s and 1990s. It was by now known to many as the

The Subway was utterly transformed with its 1970s rebuild, as shown in this present-day scene at Bridge Street. Car No. 133 leads the three-coach outer circle train. (Author's collection)

'Clockwork Orange' on account of the trains' innovative new livery and received another boost in 1992 when eight new unpowered trailer cars (numbered 201–8) joined the fleet, allowing all services to be made up of three-car rakes from that point onwards.

SPT days

The centenary of the Underground in 1996 was seen as a good opportunity to upgrade the system again, and resignalling took place. All power cars were refurbished by Adtranz in Derby but retained their all-over orange livery, now carrying the logos of their new operator Strathclyde Passenger Transport (SPT). This took them through to the new millennium, before they were repainted once again, this time into a version of the SPT carmine and cream livery to match the regular trains. Around this time, special advertising liveries also became commonplace. The trailer vehicles were subsequently overhauled at Springburn works, while 2002 saw the railway officially renamed by SPT as the 'Glasgow Subway' – its original name – instead of the 'Underground'. Other minor improvements included the addition of digital boards at stations displaying the time of the next arrival on each circle.

Recent years have seen SPT examine the feasibility of finally extending the Subway to other parts of the city and for a while it actually looked like such plans were being given some consideration. A 2007 proposal was for a new circle into the east end, which could partly make use of the remaining tunnels from the Beeching closures in that part of town. Stations would be at St Mungo's, Onslow, Duke Street, Celtic Park, Dalmarnock, Newhall and the Gorbals. However, the plan was thrown out on cost grounds, after a whopping £2.3 billion investment was quoted for the work. There is still the possibility of such a scheme in the future, but the solid bedrock under the city would be a problem for any further tunnelling.

Nevertheless, the existing Underground network is currently in the midst of getting its first major refurbishment since 1979. At a cost of £288 million, stations are being spruced up with all-new wall panels and platform paving, plus new escalators. Hillhead was the first station so treated, being fully completed with a new ticket office in 2012. The current rolling stock is also planned for replacement soon with driverless units, while fully automatic signalling is set to reduce the human operating element even further. This is a far cry from the pre-1977 era, when there was a station master who also acted as signalman at all fifteen stops on the system. Lastly, smartcard ticketing was also launched recently.

Passenger volumes on the 'Clockwork Orange' have stayed at a similar level throughout the past two decades, with generally between 13 and 14 million journeys made per year. While commuters and students form a major part of that, there are also large football crowds, with Rangers fans heading to Ibrox. A typical home match day sees a number of stewards drafted in to deal with the extra congestion and notices advising the public to avoid using the system during the early and late afternoon periods. The peak frequency of trains in general remains at every four minutes, though there is still a desire for this to be increased. Prior to the 1970s modernisation, it was not possible to alternate between peak and off-peak services due to the difficulty in moving sets to and from the depot without a connecting line.

Broomloan depot is the Subway headquarters, as it houses the overall control centre in addition to the running and repair sheds. The colour light signals are operated from here, using track circuits and panels to display train movements as on conventional rail. Part of it is also a CCTV monitoring workstation, with a wide array of cameras, gradually expanded through the years, covering every part of the network including all stations. The control centre is manned 24/7, partly because track maintenance teams work on the line every night after the day's services have finished. Three battery electric locomotives are provided for use on the permanent way trains.

13

2014 Commonwealth Games and the Railway

At the time of writing, the 2014 Commonwealth Games in Glasgow is only months away, with eleven days of competition from 23 July to 3 August 2014. This will be the first time that the gargantuan sports event has been held in Scotland's biggest city. The railway, including the Glasgow Subway, will undoubtedly be the ideal mode of transport for spectators, as it offers quick and easy access to all of the venues, which includes Hampden, Parkhead and Ibrox stadiums, Kelvingrove Park, Strathclyde Country Park and the Hydro Arena. The Athletes' Village and purpose-built Emirates Arena have also been established near Parkhead, with Dalmarnock being the nearest station.

Dalmarnock's brand-new station building; a sign of the future perhaps? (Author's collection)

Previously just a dreary, bog-standard suburban station on the Argyle line, Dalmarnock received a new lease of life with the distinction of being the gateway to the Games. It has just received the finishing touches to a massive £12 million refurbishment which, such was the extent of the work, saw it closed to the public for nearly a whole year, between 4 June 2012 and 19 May 2013. This involved the building of a brand-new frontage on Dalmarnock Road to replace the previous structure on Swanston Street. It was therefore *not* an entirely new station, despite many billing it as such. Funding was a combined effort between SPT, Glasgow City Council, Clyde Gateway, the European Regional Development Fund (ERDF) and Network Rail.

Work at Dalmarnock commenced in September 2011 and the full closure period was initially expected to be just six months, but groundwork problems caused further delays. The station is of course located in a deep cutting below street level, at the starting point of the Argyle line's underground section, with one of the two staggered platforms sitting halfway into the tunnel. Large supporting beams also span the tracks and the shadows from these only added to the gloomy atmosphere at the station through the years. These 1895-vintage Glasgow Central Railway features have been retained after the refurbishment, but new platform surfaces and wall cladding were added after cleaning and repairs were undertaken.

The new station building at Dalmarnock is of a very modern, dynamic design never seen before on the city's railways, with an elaborate zigzag roof and glass panel wall design similar to the Riverside Museum at Partick. A spacious booking hall leads to a brand-new footbridge with lifts to either platforms. The new building and ticket office were open to passengers in May 2013 but the footbridge and lifts were not available until 6 December, when the station rebuild was officially completed. Not only was it a boost for ScotRail, but Dalmarnock's facelift also contributed to the wider Glasgow east end regeneration programme that has been taking place in recent years.

With such state-of-the-art facilities, Dalmarnock was no longer such an ugly duckling and, from the outside at least, it made some of the better-looking ScotRail stations pale in comparison! But with such a big cultural event taking place in the city, Transport Scotland wanted to ensure that *all* stations in Glasgow received attention, with the idea that transport facilities would give visitors a good impression of the city as a whole.

The past few years have seen the new ScotRail Saltire train re-livery programme rapidly accelerated so as to have most multiple units in these colours by the time of the Games. At the same time, most stations in the city have had their main furnishings repainted in the uniform blue and white to replace the old SPT carmine and cream, with new nameboards in the revised typeface, complete with 'ScotRail: Scotland's Railway' branding and, in some cases, the name in Gaelic

Despite being given a dose of ScotRail 'Saltire' colours and the line being electrified, King's Park station, on the Cathcart–Newton line, has changed little since the days of steam. Here, a Class 314 leaves for Newton on a freezing November day. (Author's collection)

One 1990s straggler is Williamwood, which – for now at least – still carries a large nameboard in orange Strathclyde PTE colours across its adjoining road bridge, despite the station itself getting Saltire treatment. These large road bridge signs were once commonplace all around the city, allowing easy sighting of stations from street level. Jordanhill and Anniesland still had SPTE versions as late as 2011.

With the Homecoming and Ryder Cup events taking place in 2014 in addition to the Games, there have been other minor station upgrades. Over £2 million was ploughed into those in the Strathclyde area; the most common enhancement being the installation of LED customer information screens to replace the old TV-monitor types. Much put-upon stations like Hillfoot, Garscadden, Drumry and Coatdyke were spruced up with this modification, while Lenzie and

Anniesland got brand-new waiting rooms. As well as that, a rise in bicycle use by the general public has been noticeable in the last couple of years and thankfully more provision has been made for cyclists to combine this with train travel. Lenzie, Bishopbriggs, Dalmuir, Paisley Canal, Bellshill and Whitecraigs are soon to get new bike shelters as part of the 2014 investment.

With Transport Scotland wanting every aspect of the city's railways to be in tip-top shape for the Commonwealth Games, it was no surprise when it was announced that some of the forthcoming electrification schemes were to be accelerated to have them finished before summer 2014. The introduction of EMUs on the Paisley Canal route had demonstrated their superior acceleration to diesel units, with improved punctuality during the first six months of operation, so there was a desire for more of this as soon as possible. It was subsequently announced that work on both the Whifflet and Springburn–Cumbernauld lines would be brought forward by four years to be finished for the May 2014 timetable change. After electric services start, both aforementioned routes will join the low-level network, being served by Glasgow Central and Queen Street lower platforms respectively instead of the high-levels. The new Dalmuir–Springburn service will require a reversal at Springburn, which will add to the journey time slightly.

Anglo-Scottish traffic will also benefit from the Whifflet electrification, as the line will become another possible diversionary route in the event of engineering work. As for the WCML itself, it will be a vital artery for a large proportion

At the start of 2014, electrification of the Springburn–Cumbernauld line was at an advanced stage. A First ScotRail-liveried Sprinter is seen beneath the new catenary at Stepps on 6 January, forming the 1011 departure for Glasgow Queen Street. (Author's collection)

of visitors to the Commonwealth Games. The past five years alone have seen passenger demand grow by approximately 144 per cent between Glasgow and London Euston, hence the now hourly eleven-car Pendolinos and extra trains via Birmingham.

ScotRail are naturally planning an expanded timetable and longer trains over the July–August period as Glasgow 2014 dawns ever closer on the horizon. On some level, this busy summer can be seen as the culmination of all of the work that has gone into improving and expanding the city's rail network in general for the past few decades. This includes the Subway too, which is currently undergoing its own share of modifications for the Games. There was a drive to get smartcard ticketing in use by late 2013, while Partick, Kelvinhall and Ibrox are some of the first stations to get a full refurbishment to ensure they are ready in time for the big day.

The rail network is clearly in a better position to support an event of this scope than it would have been even, say, ten years ago, given the amount of line reopenings and service and station enhancements that have taken place since then. Travelling spectators will no doubt be impressed by the speed, reliability and good connections of the train service, not to mention some of the modern station facilities, and this is clearly the sort of thing which befits a city hosting the Commonwealth Games.

14

The Railway Today

With the 50th anniversary of the Beeching Report having just passed and a flurry of improvements for the Commonwealth Games now coming to an end, 2014 is a good time to examine the current state of play on Glasgow's railways. Lines previously closed have been reopened, with new stations built, more lines electrified, stations refurbished and capacity and service frequencies enhanced. So the question is: what now for the Strathclyde network?

The first answer most people would give is Crossrail. In a nutshell, this is the name given to a much talked about potential new rail link which would allow

The City Union Bridge across the Clyde, which could potentially open to passenger traffic as part of a Glasgow Crossrail scheme. (Author's collection)

through passenger journeys between the north and east and the south and west of Scotland without the need to change at Glasgow Queen Street and Central, that is, by crossing the Clyde. This would open up a whole new range of service possibilities, such as Edinburgh to Kilmarnock, Inverness to Stranraer or Aberdeen to Glasgow Airport, and the advantage is that there is already a linking line: the City Union line through the Gorbals, which has not seen regular passenger trains since the closure of St Enoch station.

The Crossrail plan has been under proposal for decades, first mentioned in the Greater Glasgow Transportation Survey in 1968 with the same fundamental idea of using the City Union line. As was the case back then, the closest thing to it on the existing network would be routing a train from the south via Whifflet and Coatbridge, which would be thoroughly indirect even if line capacity was available. Supporters of the proposal suggest a 'Strathbungo chord' to give the City Union line a southbound connection towards East Kilbride and Dumfries, while a revival of the 'Garngad chord' near Springburn would allow another option for trains to Edinburgh and the north. Other ideas are for a west-facing curve at High Street to access Glasgow Queen Street low-level and new stations at West Street (for a Subway connection), the Gorbals and Glasgow Cross.

Glasgow Central is around a ten-minute walk from Queen Street, through some very congested streets, and this is far from ideal for passengers with large amounts of luggage or prams. There is a shuttle bus provided between the two stations, which is free to train ticket holders, but this saves only a couple of minutes at best.

Crossrail would alleviate this problem, but critics of the scheme point out that taking the City Union route avoids the city centre, even if it would allow for quick through-journeys and a much needed new station in the Trongate area (reopening Glasgow Cross station on the Central low-level route would be another possibility). Furthermore, despite the fact that most of the infrastructure is already in place, the Scottish Government threw out the plans in 2006, believing it would not compete strongly enough with car journeys and would therefore not be worthy of such investment. The other option of some kind of underground Crossrail is unlikely due to the cost and difficulty of boring new tunnels beneath the city.

The use of a light rail network in Glasgow has also been proposed by transport groups and authorities such as Glasgow City Council, particularly for local lines south of the Clyde like the Cathcart Circle. Street-running with trams has been suggested, but road congestion could be prohibitive, and lessons have been learned from the spiralling costs of the Edinburgh tramway system, though light rail is generally cheaper to build and operate than the conventional system, as it can use the same standard-gauge track, with lower access charges, or run on roadways. The Tyne and Wear Metro railway is standard-gauge and the second largest metro system in the UK ahead of the Glasgow Subway. Its success has prompted talk of a similar system being used in Glasgow, perhaps as a long-overdue airport link.

Such is the intensity of current train services in the city that line capacity is becoming stretched. This is particularly true for the WCML along its full length, and there is furthermore talk of the future HS2 high-speed line south of the border potentially reaching Glasgow one day, with some kind of interchange station to connect it to the Crossrail scheme, plus a link to the high-speed Edinburgh–Glasgow line. If there is one drawback to high-frequency timetables, it is in the rare case of a train or signalling failure, where one incident can cause huge knock-on tailbacks with trains effectively queued up for miles until they get a clear signal, if not cancelled completely. The Finnieston–Jordanhill section of the North Clyde/Argyle lines is a perfect example of this, with trains passing through at two-minute intervals and the line pushed to capacity. The media in particular tends to be in uproar about every train cancellation or delay resulting from a situation like this, but if a fast and frequent service is desired by the public, this is the price that very occasionally has to be paid.

Electrification is still seen as the way forward for Glasgow's railways, just as it was fifty years ago. It is interesting that a lot of the projects have only started in

Two consecutive 'Big Freezes' in recent years have certainly provided a test for ScotRail. On 28 November 2010, 334037 braves a snow shower at Hyndland with a late-running service to Motherwell. (Author's collection)

recent years, as some of them were first proposed back in 1968 by the Greater Glasgow Transportation Survey, which desired a near enough all-electric network throughout the city. So perhaps the Commonwealth Games looming on the horizon has given the railway the shake-up it has long needed. The fast, seamless transport networks of other cities abroad and domestically, such as London's, have certainly set an example for Glasgow to follow.

Scotland's 2011 census reveals a large increase in car usage by commuters in the past decade and a drop in bus travel, though train usage has risen from 3 per cent of the total working population in 2001 to 4 per cent in 2011. There has also been a 30 per cent growth in ScotRail's overall passenger numbers in the past decade and a rising population should ensure this figure is kept high. This has been despite a degree of distrust from an element of the public towards the railway in recent years due to industrial strikes and continuing fare rises, but the latter is of little concern in the context of rapidly rising petrol prices that are making car travel less appealing.

The reliability of the trains themselves today can certainly not be called into question. On both the freight and passenger side, there was a period of decline through the 1990s, with a lot of reliance on ageing locomotives and multiple units, but the past fifteen years in particular have seen a massive programme of replacing most of these. In fact, today's ScotRail and Virgin fleets are almost unrecognisable compared with what was around just over a decade ago. Even the oldest passenger trains still in use – the Class 314s – are very reliable and could certainly do a job for years to come. To railfans, they represent the last of an old generation and, like the Class 303s before them, are a type indigenous to Scotland's largest city.

It is even more incredible in this day and age that even older designs – the Class 08s and 37s – still play a regular part in freight operations. The fact that these locomotives can still perform at such a high level is surely testament to the great legacy of British engineering which Glasgow was once a big part of. This does at least continue to live on in Clyde shipbuilding, while the former 'Caley' works at Springburn still carries out major repairs on locomotives.

Regarding freight, it is unfortunate that so much of the remaining traffic in the area is through-workings to destinations outside Glasgow; something which can be attributed to both the decline of local heavy industries and the move to road haulage. Mossend receives huge trainloads every day, but its location is a good distance out of town and connecting lorries still have to be driven considerable distances for the product to reach its final destination in the city. Looking back a few decades, much of the goods and raw materials used to go the whole way by train, or at least to terminals closer by within the city, meaning they only went by road for a short distance if at all; but watch this space, as they say, because growing city road congestion can still work in rail's favour.

DRS's economical and environmentally friendly 'Tesco Express' workings have certainly set a great standard in this regard which will hopefully be a template for some new operations.

Declining freight was a major reason for many of Glasgow's Beeching closures. In conclusion, it would be fair to say that the cuts were harsh on both the passenger and goods networks given the number of lines and stations which disappeared in the mid–late 1960s; a look at past and present maps reveals a once-complex spider's web of routes connecting to every residential area and dockyard in the city, replaced by what is now very much a simple but efficient railway system. Local morale was also kept up at that time by BR's publicity campaigns to highlight new trains and faster services (e.g. the 'Blue Trains'), which somewhat masked the effects of the cutbacks, unlike in some other parts of the country where there was little to cheer about.

Although the Beeching Report is usually remembered for its drastic effect on rural railways, it clearly hit the cities hard as well and one only needs to look eastwards to Edinburgh, which suffered much worse than Glasgow. The Scottish capital lost virtually all of its suburban passenger traffic in one fell swoop; at the same time, Glasgow retained the vast majority of its traffic and that is the key difference.

The busy Pollokshields East station lies adjacent to Muirhouse Junction, where both sides of the Cathcart Circle diverge separately from the main line to Kilmarnock. Trains pass by the minute, as demonstrated here with a Sprinter overtaking Class 314 No. 314202, both heading for Glasgow Central. (Author's collection)

The Clydeside rail network has recovered well from Beeching too, even if there are still a few loose ends that could be tied up, such as pushing ahead with the Crossrail scheme. The scale of line and station reopenings since has been impressive, but all at great expense, and they should never really have had to happen in the first place. The over-zealousness of BR's closures in the 1960s is all too clear to see today and Glasgow is no different from a lot of other parts of the country in this regard. In Glasgow's case, politicians of that era failed to realise the huge advantages of rail transport in and around busy urban centres, and the subsequent boom in travel that would come decades later. Obviously few could have predicted the fast and frequent passenger services of today – including a revitalised Subway system – which is the reason why so many of the public choose to take the train.

Scotland finds itself at an unusual crossroads in 2014, due to the forthcoming independence referendum. This means that on the transport front there can be no guarantees of what the future will hold. There is also the small matter of new franchises about to take over the main ScotRail passenger and sleeper operations (still in the bidding stage at the time of writing). They will have their own ideas on how they want the services to run.

Nevertheless, the future is looking bright for Glasgow's railways. Developments within the past few decades have shown that the railways still play a massive part in people's lives and, if anything, are set to expand even more, with the possibility of other closed lines or stations being reopened, so the legacy of Beeching lives on.

Sources

Books

Buck, M. & Rawlinson, M., *Line by Line: The West Coast Main Line London Euston to Glasgow Central* (Swindon: Freightmaster, 2000)

Cameron, D., *Glasgow Central, Central to Glasgow* (Boat of Garten: Strathwood, 2006)

Cross, D., *The Heyday of the Scottish Diesels* (Hersham: Ian Allan, 2002)

Hodgins, D. & Sanders, K., *British Railways Past and Present: No. 31 North West Scotland* (Kettering: Past and Present Publishing, 1998)

Martin, D. & MacLean, A.A., *Edinburgh & Glasgow Railway Guidebook* (Glasgow: Strathkelvin District Libraries & Museums, 1992)

Millar, A., *British PTEs: 1, Strathclyde* (London: Ian Allan, 1985)

Morrison, G., *Scottish Railways Then & Now* (Shepperton, Surrey: Ian Allan, 1999)

Noble, T., *Profile of the Class 26s and 27s* (Oxford: OPC, 1982)

Sellar, W.S. & Stevenson, D.L., *Last Trains: (2) Glasgow & Central Scotland* (Edinburgh: Moorfoot, 1980)

Smith, W.A.C., *Renfrewshire's Last Days of Steam*, (Catrine, Ayrshire: Stenlake, 2002)

Smith, W.A.C. & Anderson, P., *An Illustrated History of Glasgow's Railways* (Oldham: Irwell Press, 1993)

Watson, G., *Glasgow Subway Album* (Chetwode, Buckingham: Adam Gordon, 2000)

Welch, M.S., *Diesels over the Roof of England* (Settle: Waterfront, 2003)

Websites

www.railscot.co.uk

www.canmore.rcahms.gov.uk (Royal Commission on the Ancient and Historical Monuments of Scotland)

www.networkrail.co.uk

www.networkrailmediacentre.co.uk
www.railwaysarchive.co.uk
www.scot-rail.co.uk
www.scotrail.co.uk
www.signallingnotices.org.uk
www.spt.co.uk
www.therailengineer.com
www.6lda.wordpress.com

National Archives of Scotland

BR/LIB/S/4/213 – *100 Years of the Central: History of Glasgow Central Station*, 1979

BR/LIB/S/15/274 – Council of Engineering Institutions: *Trans-Clyde: A Private Preview for Professional Engineers, Modernisation of BR's Argyle Line and the Greater Glasgow Passenger Transport Executive Underground*, September 1979. With copies of *Underground News, Nos. 1 and 2 of Trans-Clyde News*, and leaflet *Strathclyde's strategy for transport transformation: Glasgow's Clockwork Orange*

BR/RSR/4/169 – BR Scottish Region: *Glasgow Central Station Platform Arrangements*, 1973

BR/RSR/4/278 – BR Scottish Region: *Permanent Way and Signalling Arrangements: Glasgow Central Signalling Centre*

BR/RSR/4/334 – BR Scottish Region: *Permanent Way and Signalling Arrangements for Glasgow Central Signalling Centre: Extension of Area of Control*, 1973

BR/RSR/4/975 – *System Analysis of Signal Boxes Operating in British Railways Scottish Region*, 1971–75

GD344/3/35 – BR Scottish Region: *Platform arrangements at Glasgow Central Station and Glasgow Fair Holiday arrangements, including special traffic notices and guards' programmes*, 30 May–27 Sept 1970

GD482/142 – British Rail: *Queen St. Station of the 70s*, 1973

RCC4/9 – Transport Users Consultative Committtee for Scotland: Meeting of Committee, 27 Jan 1971

East Renfrewshire Council Archives

GB 3143 – Glasgow-East Kilbride Railway Development Association, 1973–1990: Nos 6/01, 6/05, 6/12, 6/22, 6/27, 7/2, 8/19, 8/23, 8/27, 9/2

Other

City of Glasgow District Council Planning Department: *Options for the Glasgow Rail Network*, January 1987

Department of Transport: *Report of the Inquiry into the Collision at Bellgrove Junction on 6 March 1989*

Glasgow City Council: *Keep Glasgow Moving: Draft Consultation – April 1998*

Glasgow's New Underground, written by J.H. Price and reprinted from *Modern Tramway*, published by Light Rail Transit Association

Greater Glasgow Transportation Study Volume V: *1978–85 Investment Programme for Transportation in the Greater Glasgow Area*

Strathclyde Passenger Transport: *Underground Centenary 1896–1996*, 1996

Various British Rail working timetables (WTTs), public timetables and publicity leaflets

Various *MacBac* Air, Rail and Steamer timetables

Magazines and Newspapers

Blastpipe (Scottish Railway Preservation Society journal)
Carrick Gazette
Entrain
Evening Times
The Herald
Model Rail
Motive Power Monthly
Rail
The Railway Magazine
Railways Illustrated
The Scotsman
Scottish Transport (Scottish Tramway Museum Society journal)
Traction

Video & DVD

The Railways of Scotland Volume Ten: Glasgow Part Two (Cinerail, 1998)
The Railway Monthly: Issue 2, July 2004 (Brainwave Media Ltd, 2004)

Index